Wittgenstein and Buddhism

WITTGENSTEIN
AND
BUDDHISM

Chris Gudmunsen

BARNES & NOBLE
BOOKS
10 East 53d St., New York 10022
(a division of Harper & Row Publishers, Inc.)

First published 1977 by
THE MACMILLAN PRESS LTD
London and Basingstoke

Published in the U.S.A. 1977 by
HARPER & ROW PUBLISHERS, INC.
BARNES & NOBLE IMPORT DIVISION

ISBN 0-06-492585-4

Library of Congress Catalog Card Number: 76-19863

Printed in Great Britain

Contents

Preface

What one might expect at the beginning of a book of this kind is an expression of regret that Eastern and Western philosophy, not having grown up together, are still shy on meeting. Very well: it is regrettable. It is true that they often seem to have dishearteningly little in common, but that makes it all the more exciting on the odd occasion when it is realised that much the same thing has been going on quite independently on both sides of Istanbul. I suppose that it would be more exciting still if it could be established that Wittgenstein's later work was *not* independent of Buddhist philosophy. But I shall be arguing in the last chapter that such a view, even though not wildly stupid, cannot really be correct.

The similarities between Wittgenstein and Buddhism, then, are fortuitous. This raises a question about what exactly I am trying to do in the following chapters and what would and would not be a valid method of doing it. Edward Conze, for instance, in an article called 'Spurious Parallels to Buddhist Philosophy' says that spurious parallels

> often originate from a wish to find affinities with philosophers recognized and admired by the exponents of current academic philosophy, and intend to make Buddhist thinkers interesting and respectable by current Western standards. Since this approach is not only objectively unsound, but has also failed in its purpose to interest Western philosophers in the philosophies of the East, the time has now come to abandon it.[1]

It seems to me, on the other hand, that this view expressed by Conze has become an orthodoxy in Buddhist studies and that the time has now come to abandon *it* or at least to move on from it a little. What I wish to do is precisely that which is condemned by Conze. I do wish to find affinities with a philosopher recognised and admired by some exponents of current academic philosophy, though that is not all. Various recent academic philosophers, not least Wittgenstein, have had a considerable impact upon Christian theology, and there is no reason why the same should not apply to the Buddhist equivalent of Christian theology. But which, it might be asked, am I trying to do? Am I saying that Wittgenstein and certain schools of Buddhist philosophy were saying much the same thing; or am I offering a new interpretation of those schools in accordance with Wittgensteinian ideas? The answer is that I am doing both. The reason why the second does not invalidate the first is because, as I shall be arguing, only a Wittgensteinian interpretation will suffice for certain central Buddhist concepts. In other words, Buddhist philosophy once took a markedly Wittgensteinian turn.

In that same article of Conze's, he suggests four aspects of philosophical doctrines which need to be borne in mind to avoid spurious parallels. There is the formulation of certain propositions, the motives and purposes of the author, the kinds of arguments they use and the context in which the statements are made. I have, I hope, dealt satisfactorily with the first three, but the last – 'a context which is determined by the philosopher's predecessors and contemporaries, and by his social, cultural and religious background'[2] – simply cannot, of course, apply here. The two contexts in question could hardly be more different; that is partly what makes the whole thing so interesting.

Interesting to whom, though? In view of the prevailing East-West philosophical apartheid there will, presumably, be two fairly distinct groups of readers of this book. To those interested more in Wittgenstein than in Buddhism I have nothing philosophically startling to say (although perhaps some of Wittgenstein's ideas may have a slightly different flavour after being set alongside similar ideas differently expressed). Any interest for them will be aroused largely by the novelty of the historical coincidences. Readers of Wittgenstein do not normally suffer from *déjà vu* because they have never seen any reason to regard Buddhist philosophy as relevant to their concerns, perhaps regarding it as too tainted by mysticism or devotionalism to be hard-headed and painstaking. I hope that this will be seen to be a false dichotomy in this case. Those whose interest lies in Buddhism rather than in Wittgenstein will be familiar with parallels, spurious and otherwise, which have been held to obtain between Buddhism and Western philosophy. But apart from offering yet more of these, I have tried to show that academic philosophy can help to clarify religious statements. The approach of a modern Western philosopher often means trouble for the Christian theologian, who is not infrequently left with the feeling that his beliefs have been somehow demeaned. Buddhists have, I think, less to fear. If this is so, it has probably something to do with the fact that Buddhism has, for most of its life, been much more overtly philosophical than has Christianity. At all events, the school of Mahāyāna Buddhism with which I shall be chiefly concerned – the Mādhyamika – has least of all to fear, since it represents philosophical Buddhism par excellence.

To those interested in both Buddhism *and* Wittgenstein, I assume that I need say nothing at all.

C.G.

Acknowledgements

The author and publishers wish to thank Basil Blackwell and Mott Ltd, Oxford, for kindly granting permission to use extracts from *The Blue and Brown Books* and *Philosophical Investigations* by Ludwig Wittgenstein.

Part One

RUSSELL AND THE ABHIDHARMISTS

1 Logic

Philosophy in the grand style requires plenty of capital letters: Being, the Self, Substance, Reality and so on. Its practitioners have to construct metaphysical systems and deal with cosmology. The truths about the universe are large, static, universal Truths on which particular facts of experience have little bearing. The Truths have a religious flavour; discovering them is a job for sages. Philosophy is constructive, not critical. Just such heavy, elaborate, authoritarian ways of thinking were the prevailing philosophical orthodoxies against which early Buddhism and Russell reacted. That their reactions led to some very similar philosophical conclusions was not, I think, a matter of similar reactions to similar orthodoxies, because the respective orthodoxies (the Brāhmanical tradition and neo-Hegelian Idealism) were not similar except in the rather general way I have indicated.

The similarities I am going to point out do not refer, of course, to the entire philosophies of Russell and Buddhism. Russell's epistemology from about 1911 to 1914, with some ideas from his logical atomism, are what I shall be dealing with. On the Buddhist side, I shall not be much concerned with the period before the formation of schools with their own scriptures, partly because not enough is known and partly because what is known does not suggest a detailed and systematic philosophy. That part of the scriptures of Hīnayāna schools which does deal with philosophy in a detailed way is the *Abhidharma*. There are not enormous differences between the views of Abhidharmists of different schools, but enough to make it convenient to consider a particular school. Here, it will be mainly the *Sarvāstivāda*, a school whose Abhidharma takes to satisfyingly extreme lengths the tendencies, especially in ontology, found in the Abhidharma generally. And since the Abhidharma is itself meant to be the taking to logical conclusions and quintessence of the basic popular scriptures, the Sutras, the Sarvāstivādin Abhidharmists present a nice clear case. Perhaps partly for this reason, it is the Sarvāstivāda whose theories came in for particular attack from the Mahāyāna. The Theravāda, though now the only remaining Hīnayāna school, was of rather slight importance in the history of philosophy.

Particulars, Qualities and Dharmas

The truth about the world is found, according to Russell and the

Sarvāstivāda, not by looking for ever larger and more inclusive statements about general states of affairs, but by looking for small, precise statements about individually unexciting yet incontrovertible facts. Analysis, not construction yields ultimate facts. It is difficult, when dealing with either Russell or the Sarvāstivādins, wholly to separate logic, ontology and epistemology, because the ingredients of the ultimate facts are what really exist and are also what are known by acquaintance. None the less, I want to deal first with the logical status of the real objects in the world.

For Russell and the Sarvāstivādins the only respectable use of language is the kind of statement which gives descriptions of what is the case. Descriptions of what is the case can be reduced to simple descriptions of simple objects. The simple objects exist, and are in fact all that exists. What does exist, then; what are the simple objects? There are *particulars* which have *qualities* of one sort or another and stand in *relations* to each other. The logical simplicity of all three is ensured for Russell by making none dependent on the other. A particular has qualities and relations but it could have quite different qualities or stand in quite different relations to other particulars without being a different particular. Similarly, a quality or relation cannot be defined as being the quality or relation pertaining to a certain particular. Even if two simple particulars were of a certain unique colour and bore a unique relation to each other, the quality and relation would continue to exist in some sense even if the two particulars ceased to exist. This has the strange consequence that even though one can recognise a particular only by its properties, it has no properties intrinsically.

According to Russell, proper names can be given only, strictly, to existents. As a result, it turned out that very few proper names are possible. This is because, if a name helps to *describe* the particular in any way, the name must be purged of all descriptive content by shelving it on to predicates one can apply to it. If one starts with a particular whose name is suspiciously descriptive one has to give the particular a simpler, less descriptive name and say that this particular has such and such properties. Continuing the process, one is left with only 'this' and 'that' as ideal names.

In the Abhidharma, all simple objects are known as *dharmas*. In the various schools, lists of dharmas are given which differ from each other, but not in any crucial way. The Sarvāstivādins had a list of 75 dharmas, which constitute an inventory of the entire furniture of the universe, as Russell would say. It is left unstated, by the Abhidharmists as well as by Russell, whether or not the number of pieces of furniture is infinite, but at all events it is a lot greater than 75, which makes it clear that the list of 75 dharmas is some sort of classification. The word 'dharma' has to serve as a term both for particulars and their qualities.[1] (I shall deal with relations later.) This happened because the dharma-theory was an attempt to do what Russell did in *An Enquiry into Meaning and Truth* a number of years after he held the views considered here. That is, an attempt was made to reduce particulars entirely to sets of qualities. Stcherbatsky says, 'To every unit of quality there corresponds a dharma.'[2] But at the same time, 'whatsoever exists is a substance.' The Abhidharmists tried to be thoroughgoing in their rejection of substance with no qualities. Already common-sense 'things' – people, chairs, etc. – had been reduced to dharmas, and they also wanted to eliminate the distastefully 'substantial' aspect of dharmas themselves. But they could only bring themselves to say, 'There are no particulars, only qualities – and they are all particulars!' Their attempt, in other words, failed.

That is why the word 'dharma' refers ambiguously both to particulars and to qualities. The dharma-list is a list of 75 qualities, and of each of them there are numerous examples (particulars). Hate, for instance, is a dharma. Examples of hatred in different people are never suggested to be *united* in any way in a single particular. The 75 dharmas (as qualities) are types of dharmas (as particulars). Of course, as with Russell's 'simple particulars', the only way of identifying a dharma is by its properties. Suppose you are meditating, watching all that of which you are aware, and analysing it into simple objects, dharmas. One of the items you are aware of is hate, but then the mood goes and you are not aware of hate any longer. Of that particular item, what can you say? 'It was hate' – Yes, that was its quality. 'And at the time I said to myself, "this is hate".' – Well, the 'this' is the nearest you can get to indicating its particularity.

This distinction between dharma as particular and as quality is obviously inescapable, given a list of 75 dharmas *and* the wish to have a much larger number of dharmas than 75. But I would not like the distinction to be thought of as a belated tidying up by me of an ancient but messy philosophy. The Abhidharmists, I want to argue, were themselves obliged to draw the distinction. Let us start by considering the fact that dharmas have 'marks' (lakṣaṇa). A mark is the property of a dharma which enables one to say what type (of the 75) it is. Dharmas are 'kept apart' by their distinctive and defining properties – their 'marks'. Each of the 75 dharma-types has a mark to help one identify it as such. Jayatilleke gives as examples:

> 'Greed' has the characteristic [= mark] of wanting... 'Desire' has the characteristic of attachment... 'Absence of hatred' has the characteristic of not harming... Here lakkhaṇa [Pāli for lakṣaṇa, mark] is used to denote the 'basic characteristic' of a concept which

> distinguishes it from everything else, but in the section on lakkhaṇa, the term is used in the sense of a 'property' common to members of a class . . . These two 'senses' are basically the same in that the essential characteristic of a thing is a property common to members of the class to which it belongs.[3]

The Abhidharmists were not unaware of the fact that names of dharmas sometimes had to denote universals. There was, for instance, disagreement[4] between the Theravāda and the 'Rājagirikas and Siddhattikas', who were sub-sects of the Mahāsaṇghikas, the main Hīnayāna precursor of the Mahāyāna. The Mahāsaṇghika position was that 'there do not exist any dharmas which can be grouped together by other dharmas.' The Theravāda reply was that pleasure, pain and neutral feelings must surely fall under the heading 'feelings' (vedanā). Jayatilleke comments that this is 'one of the earliest references to universals',[5] and it may represent a beginning of the Mahāyāna dissatisfaction with one of the Hīnayāna assumptions about dharmas.

But how did the Abhidharmists speak of the fact that a dharma as particular is logically separate from its marks, its properties? How did the Sarvāstivādins, who tried, as we shall see, to extend the life of a dharma a little longer than the 'instant' usual in most schools, make it clear that they were referring to a particular lasting through time and not to a timeless universal or quality? They did it by using the phrase 'a dharma's own-being' (dharma-svabhāva). A dharma's own-being is what carries its 'own-mark' (svalakṣaṇa). All references to a dharma's 'own-being' are references to its actually existing. The Sarvāstivāda, for example, argue that in an absolute sense (paramārtha), all dharmas have own-being, because otherwise when one dharma was produced or ceased, so would all other conditioned dharmas. When Mahāyānists denied dharmas' own-being, they were denying the real existence of dharmas as it had been conceived by the Abhidharmists. 'What has no own-being, that is non-existent.'[6]

According to the Sarvāstivādins, one is aware of a dharma only in the present while it has its mark, yet it can exist 'markless' (i.e. with no descriptive content) both before and after this. They make a clear distinction between a dharma's own-being, which lasts through time, and its being identifiable at a particular moment by its mark.[7]

Russell never drew up a list of all possible simple properties (i.e. qualities and relations), like the Abhidharmists' dharma-lists. A. J. Ayer, however, has pointed out that, for Russell

> the criterion for the simplicity of an object lies in the simplicity of the properties which are attributable to it. We have already seen

that a difficulty arises from the fact that, with a little ingenuity, we can represent any property as a conjunction or disjunction of other properties. I do not know how this is going to be met except by simply listing the predicates which we are going to count as primitive. To answer Russell's requirements, these predicates must be so chosen that the properties for which they stand are absolutely specific, homogeneous, and directly exemplified within our experience.[8]

To answer the Abhidharmists' requirements, the predicates *were* so chosen that the properties for which they stood were absolutely specific, homogeneous and directly exemplified within our experience. If Russell *had* drawn up such a list, notice, it could only have been, like the dharma-list, a list of properties, not of particulars. One can describe particulars only in the sense that one can set out their properties. Apart from that, one can only use demonstrative pronouns.

Relations

We have seen how dharmas have qualities, even though the ideas of 'universal' and 'inhering quality' have often been pointed out as having been firmly rejected by the Abhidharmists. I shall now make some comparable remarks about relations. In both these points I set myself against Stcherbatsky, who has said,

> The objective reality of substance has been denied in Europe . . . in our own days by Bertrand Russell, for whom substances are not 'permanent bits of matter' but 'brief events', however possessing qualities and relations. For the Buddhist, we have seen, they are instantaneous events without qualities and relations in them.[9]

Having argued that dharmas, like Russellian particulars, have *qualities*, I hope to show that dharmas also stand in *relations* to one another, and that these relations are external to the particular (as Russell held). I also hope to show that, as was the case with qualities, these claims are not merely claims about possible interpretations but are forced on us by the statements of the Abhidharmists themselves.

For Russell, relations are objects and are real, but their ontological status, while hovering near existence, is dubious. He says,

> Suppose, for instance, that I am in my room. I exist and my room exists; but does 'in' exist? Yet obviously the word 'in' has a meaning; it denotes a relation which holds between me and my room. This relation is something, although we cannot say that it exists *in the same sense* in which I and my room exist.[10]

Relations . . . must be placed
in a world which is neither mental nor physical.[11]

You see how the argument in the first quoted passage works: 'in' has a meaning, so it must denote an object. This is exactly what the Sarvāstivādins did. There is a group of dharmas (14 of the 75) which are rūpa-citta-viprayukta-saṃskāra, which means, roughly, 'dharmas neither physical nor mental'. The Sarvāstivāda alone as a school had this category. What is contained in it which compelled them to create a classification of objects which are neither physical nor mental? I quote Guenther: 'In the creation of this group there has been operative a law of projection . . . which prompted them to consider the relations that obtain between facts when they are rendered as propositions as something like "real objects".'[12] The Abhidharmists, then, not only made relations into real existents, but hived them off completely from, as one might say, the logical space between particulars which is their natural habitat.

What led Russell and the Sarvāstivādins to making entities even out of such non-concrete things as relations? I think I can best start by pointing out how central is the idea of a correspondence theory of truth for both British and Buddhist analysts. The simplest approach is to say that a sentence is true if it corresponds to a fact. For Russell, beliefs and statements are true if they correspond to facts;[13] that is, broadly, if facts are believed or stated. In the Hīnayāna Sūtras, truth is similarly defined. Jayatilleke points out[14] that truth is defined in terms of correspondence with fact. He quotes, for instance, 'When in fact there is a next world, the belief occurs to me that there is a next world, that would be a true belief.'[15]

That seems quite palatable, but the difficulties start when a 'correspondence theory' of a sort is also used as a theory of meaning for fully-analysed expressions. Russell certainly held that analysis must lead to the discovery of simple expressions, and that their *meanings* are the simple objects we have been discussing – particulars, relations and qualities. If a simple expression has meaning, there is a corresponding simple object. This works well enough for particulars but leads to a strange ontology when applied to their properties. Yet Russell needed to link up language and the world in some way. In *Principia Mathematica* he had constructed what was intended to be a logically perfect language whose syntax corresponded exactly to the 'logical form' of simple facts. But a vocabulary of terms signifying existents was necessary if the language was to be significant as well as logically perfect. Unfortunately, Russell made the meaning of *all* expressions other than purely logical ones dependent on the existence of corresponding objects.

For the Abhidharmists, there is no such clearly worked out theory. But there are clues in the dharma-theory itself that the positing of strange existents like relations was also based on a certain view of language. Most of the dharmas in the dharma-list are the kind of object one would expect to find in an analysis of experience. There is matter, sense-data and a long list of 'mental states'. But the Abhidharmists seemed dissatisfied with only 'atomic experiences', because there are also, as Guenther said, 'the relations that obtain between facts when they are rendered as propositions.'

Not only do I need expressions for my fully-analysed experiences, but I also need to be able to say that they are related to each other by being 'my' experiences. Here the Sarvāstivādins introduced 'prāpti', the binding together of all 'my' dharmas into one 'stream' (santāna). Russell, incidentally, also attempted in later years to replace a substantial ego with a relation between 'my' experiences of particulars. He calls it 'compresence, a relation which holds between any two simultaneous contents of a given mind, as well as between any two events which overlap in physical space-time.'[16] Another need for relations occurs because 'experiential' dharmas are subject to origination, disappearance, etc. and this cannot be expressed within purely experiential expressions. (I use the term 'experiential' for the dharmas which are the fully-analysed particulars of experience.) Relations between experiential dharmas such as these fall under the heading of 'neither physical nor mental'.

And that is not all: the very fact that words have meanings is itself 'dharmified'. In the 'neither physical nor mental' class there are nāma-kāya, pada-kāya and vyanjana-kāya, translated by Stcherbatsky as, respectively, 'the force imparting significance to words . . . to sentences . . . to articulate sounds.'[17] Not only the relations between particulars were represented, then, but also the relations between particulars and their corresponding expressions!

That nāma-kāya, for instance, is in no way an 'experiential dharma' is shown, not only by the fact that it is neither physical nor mental, but also by the listing of *saṃjña* as a mental dharma. 'Saṃjña' is the dharma-name corresponding to the experience of privately conferring a name on a sensation, recognising it as being of the same kind as others falling under that name, and loading up the sensation with all the emotional and other prejudices corresponding to the name. Since saṃjña obviously takes care of the experiental aspects of naming, there need be no temptation to regard nāma-kāya as experiential too. In fact, *none* of the 'neither physical nor mental' dharmas can have been arrived at by meditating on the contents of one's mind; they are not mental at all. I can see no other explanation for their being regarded as real save Guenther's.

Evaluations

The process of arguing from meaningful expressions to existent objects was extended by the Abhidharmists to an area which made Western analysts nervous. I am referring to the possible existent objects corresponding to meaningful expressions of evaluation. G. E. Moore shared Russell's analytical approach, was overwhelmingly influential in Russell's early opinions on philosophical ethics, but was not worried by non-empirical propositions. He held the view that there are ethical facts which cannot be reduced to simpler empirical facts. One can ascribe a quality of a certain unanalysable sort to objects, people, and so on. There is a ('non-natural') unanalysable quality corresponding to the word 'good', just as there is a ('natural') unanalysable quality corresponding to the word 'yellow'.

It will come as no surprise to find that the Abhidharmists made what philosophers nowadays might call 'evaluations' into dharmas. There are two noticeable, though rather dissimilar examples of this. The first occurs only in the Theravādins' dharma-list. In the category of 'mental states', there appear three dharmas called 'abstinence (virati) from bodily . . . from verbal . . . and from mental misconduct (duccarita).'[18] These three abstinences are equivalent to the 'course of karmically skilful conduct' (kusala-kamma-patha), which in turn is equivalent to virtue or morality (sīla). That the abstinences fall under the heading of 'mental states' (saṃskāras) shows that bodily and verbal misconduct are not merely physical abstinences and that abstinence from mental misconduct is not simply an absence of bad thoughts. They are evidently morally good mental states. Buddhaghosa's *Visuddhimagga*, a main Theravādin Abhidharmist work, makes it quite clear: the three abstinences 'should be regarded as the mind's averseness from evil-doing.'[19] So these three dharma-names correspond to the identifiable *experience*, the 'private sensation' if you like, of being morally good.

The *second* example of a dharma bound up with evaluation is rather different. In all Buddhist schools, conditioned dharmas are divided into five groups or, literally, heaps (skandhas). There is *citta*, consciousness, pure subjectivity with no content; the *saṃskāras*, mental states, and also, for the Sarvāstivāda, 'states neither physical nor mental'; *rūpa*, matter; *saṃjña*, as mentioned above; and *vedanā*, feelings.

Now I shall argue that vedanā has been made a separate dharma because it is, in a certain sense, evaluative. It expresses pro- and con-attitudes towards the experiencing of other dharmas. What gives us the clue to this is a pair of words with apparently similar meanings. One is *sukha* (variously translated as 'pleasure', 'happiness', 'bliss', 'ease') which falls under the skandha vedanā (feelings). Sukha is one of the three possible feelings we can have towards things, the other two being duḥkha (pain, suffering – the opposite of sukha) and upekṣā (neither sukha nor duḥkha – indifferent feelings). The other word is *pīti* (translated again as 'pleasure' or 'happiness', or sometimes as 'joy', 'zest', 'rapture' and 'interest'). Pīti is one of the many saṃskāras (identifiable mental states or 'private sensations'), so that sukha and pīti, the two kinds of pleasure – or so it seems – are members of different 'heaps' or skandhas.

Sukha and pīti are puzzling in several ways. Considering the number of different states which were subsumed under the 'mental states' heading, it is not obvious why 'feelings' or its three components should not have been too. And what is the difference between sukha and pīti? Pīti is a separate dharma, sukha is not – it is only one facet of the single dharma 'feelings'. To make matters worse, the distinction between sukha and pīti, which seems never to have been satisfactorily explained, is evidently of considerable importance in Buddhist meditation. The four trances or dhyānas are a central part of meditative practice. In the *first* trance, one is separated from sense-desires and unskilled (akauśalya) dharmas, and there are four attending states – the settling of the mind on some new 'tasty' idea (vitarka), the reflections and thoughts all around this idea (vicāra), pīti and sukha. Sukha is the only one of these which is a feeling; the rest are 'mental states'. The *second* trance occurs with the dropping of 'settling on tasty ideas' and 'thinking around them'; the *third* with the dropping of pīti and the *fourth* with the subsequent dropping of sukha.

But since we do not know the difference between pīti and sukha, what must be an important distinction for those who practise the trances is, for us, blurred over and confused. I think, however, that all these difficulties can be resolved by first considering the English word 'pleasure'. There has been some philosophical debate about whether or not pleasure is a kind of sensation. It is logically possible, that is, involves no self-contradiction, to say of any sensation that I like or dislike it. But at least part of our use of 'pleasure' is to express 'liked experience'. There is no point in arguing about whether the 'correct' use of the word 'pleasure' is as a name for a sensation or as a way of talking about the experiences I like. We use the word in both ways.[20] The ascetic may well dislike certain sensations which he and others would call pleasures (certain sense-pleasures for instance), yet one could also say that he derived pleasure from putting aside interest in pleasure. Pleasure as an identifiable sensation is, I am assuming for now, something objectively real of which one may (but possibly may not) be aware. In this sense the word 'pleasure' is descriptive, a name referring to an object in the world. In the other sense, pleasure is not an object of which I may become aware; it indicates that I *like* an object of which I am aware. The evaluative element in the 'what I like' sense is indicated by the fact that the persistent question 'what is good about X?' is brought to a halt by 'it gives me pleasure', where this is taken to mean 'I like it'. One *can* go on to ask 'what is good about pleasure?', but only if pleasure is assumed to be something to which one can react in more than one way, and then we are back with the first, 'plain sensation' sense again. To say 'I like X' is to evaluate X positively (as opposed to having disvalued X). I offer no new information about a thing if I say I like it; I rate it highly in a certain way, I consider that there is something good about it.

Pīti, I suggest, is pleasure as an experiential dharma, as an objectifiable sensation. Sukha is pleasure in the evaluative sense. What reasons are there for thinking this?

(a) Sukha is not a separate dharma; it is not a separate objectifiable sensation. Pīti is.

(b) The three feelings comprising the single dharma 'feelings' are quite different from each other, yet combine to form a single dharma. This makes sense if we think of 'feelings' (vedanā) as the evaluating or rating of other dharmas. There is only *one kind* of evaluating process in this dharma. Evaluating as 'liked' is not a kind of evaluation different from evaluating as 'disliked' or 'indifferent'. To like, dislike or be indifferent to any sensation is not to have another kind of sensation. That is why 'feelings' cannot come under the heading of 'mental states' (saṃskāras).

(c) Part of the stock analysis[21] of duḥkha (suffering, pain) is 'not to get what one wants', and sukha, its opposite,[22] means 'to get what one wants'. These are close enough to 'what I like (and . . . dislike)' to provide some confirmation.

(d) Nirvāṇa is sukha,[23] but is certainly not pīti, a conditioned dharma. This is comprehensible only if 'sukha' is not a descriptive term at all. According to my suggestion, to say that Nirvāṇa is sukha is one way of rating it highly, although there are other ways of course. Nirvāṇa could be, and often is, commended as having nothing to do with moral faults of any kind. To say it is sukha means that it is liked rather than disliked.

(e) According to Buddhaghosa,[24] where there is pīti, there is sukha [i.e. one normally likes pleasure-sensations]; but where there is sukha, there is not necessarily pīti, [i.e. one can cherish, value and like all kinds of sensations other than the sensation of pleasure].

(f) In the same passage, we are told that pīti is what an exhausted man has when told of water and shade nearby. [One could hardly say he was liking them yet, but he would have 'internal sensations' of pleasure at the thought.] But when he uses the water and feels the shade, then he has sukha; [he likes them].

Buddhaghosa also tells us[25] that pīti is of different kinds; minor pīti is only able to raise the hairs on the body, showering pīti breaks over the body again and again like waves on the sea-shore, and so on. Nothing could be more of a separate sensation than that! Sukha, however, only intensifies associated dharmas;[26] it provides no new content to our experience.

If I am right about the Hīnayāna ideas of pīti and sukha and the nature of vedanā (feelings), there are two useful by-products worth mentioning in passing. The third trance is marked by the absence of sensations of pleasure, which are now seen as distasteful and getting in the way.[27] Passing into the fourth trance occurs when one stops having a liking or disliking reaction to other dharmas which are still arising. It is not quite the case that 'feelings' are relinquished, because one still has indifferent feelings towards the other dharmas, but the existence of certain pro- and con-attitudes is destroyed.

The other point is that some light is shed on the famous statement that everything this side of Nirvāṇa is duḥkha – or 'all conditioned dharmas are duḥkha'. If duḥkha is interpreted solely as 'pain-sensation', however broad in scope this is meant to be, the statement appears simply false. As one matures, one becomes able to regard duḥkha as increasingly nearly universal, and it is easy to take refuge in this fact, saying, 'I suppose such people gradually realise that what they once found pleasant was in fact unpleasant.' But this is to miss the point. What such people do is to evaluate experience differently – they come less and less to like ordinary experience, or to cherish it, or to value it. There is no need for them to keep revising what they think is the case about the world – 'The conditioned world is wholly duḥkha; I never realised that before' – because all that happens is that they evaluate the same facts differently. We are frequently told that insight into the conditioned world's being duḥkha (that is, insight into the first 'Holy Truth') is gained fully only by the enlightened. But there is an inclination to argue with it by saying 'It's *not* all suffering; there is pleasure too.' That, however, was never denied. The point of the first Holy Truth is to describe not empirical fact but the way in which the ordinary world is evaluated from the standpoint of Nirvāṇa.

To return to the main thread, it will be seen that, unlike the three 'abstinences' of the Theravādins, vedanā has nothing to do with *moral* goodness and badness, even though it is evaluative. It would be a complete mistake, therefore, to look for any parallels here with subjectivism or prescriptivism in modern philosophical ethics. What is interesting, however, is that for Russell liking and disliking would be counted as mental facts; what is liked and disliked being a series of unanalysable particulars, sense-data. For the Abhidharmists, the rating or evaluating of other dharmas *is itself made into a simple object*, a dharma. It is put into a separate category (i.e. vedanā) to show that it is logically separate from experiential dharmas (sense-data and mental states) which are the objects of the liking and disliking.

Summary

Before going on to considerably less dry matters of epistemology in the next chapter, I shall sum up the main Russellian/Abhidharmist parallels in logic and ontology which have been looked at in this chapter.

(a) If a (non-logical) expression has meaning, there is an existing object corresponding to the expression. This remains true whether the 'object' is:

(i) Experienceable as a separate object (Russellian mental states and sense-data; experiential dharmas).

(ii) Not experienceable as a separate object because evaluative (Russellian non-natural qualities à la Moore; vedanā).

(iii) Not experienceable as a separate object because the original expression is of a relation (Russellian relations; dharmas neither physical nor mental).

(b) Tied up with (a) is the idea that the only philosophically respectable use of language is of the kind which gives descriptions of what is the case.

(c) There are simple unanalysable particulars; which boils down to saying that: There are particulars (or 'dharmas in their own-being') having in themselves no descriptive content, but which have simple, unanalysable qualities (lakṣaṇa), which are 'absolutely specific, homogeneous and directly exemplified within our experience.'

(d) The relations obtaining between particulars exist, but are neither physical nor mental.

(e) All statements about the world can be reduced by analysis to statements about particulars, qualities and relations, which are, consequently, all that exist.

2 Experience and its Objects

Sense-data

The term 'sense-datum' has been used in so many different ways that it is perhaps worth pointing out what is necessarily implied by the use of it. A sense-datum must be a datum. That is, it must be *given* to something or someone; and it must be given by the senses. It is always assumed that sense-data, whatever their nature, are sufficient to provide a complete account of what is sensed. There are two very different approaches to the significance of the term 'sense-datum', which I shall explain in reverse historical order.

One approach is to say that sense-datum language does not provide a metaphysically superior description of the world, but is just a way of talking about *how objects appear*. Sense-datum statements, on this view, are incorrigible, but at the cost of saying nothing new. If it appears to me that I see green grass, I am necessarily 'having a green sense-datum'. Sense-data are not independent objects. Still less are they objects of a new kind discovered by skilful men who have taken a very careful look (and careful smell, taste etc.) at how things appear. Sense-datum language tells us nothing different from what we are told by statements about how things appear. So sense-data cannot be more real than common sense objects.

The other approach to sense-data is a metaphysical one. They are nearer to reality than are the common-sense things we construct from them. They are a *new kind of object* which no modern universe can do without, and were discovered by skilful men. Sense-datum language is superior to our normal way of talking about things. It says more, by giving finer detail (about the new objects) and also less, by cutting out assumptions (that come with the use of ordinary language) about common-sense things – assumptions, that is, not based simply on what is sense-given.

The second, metaphysical approach is common to Russell and the Abhidharmists. Russell identified the 'particulars' we met in the last chapter most conspicuously with sense-data of this kind. The other objects with which we can be acquainted will be dealt with later. But for now let us look at sense-data.

(a) *Physical* Russell's sense-data are physical entities. Common-sense things are not analysed into our 'mental images' of their appearance, but into physical sense-data, like patches of colour, of which we can be aware. The Sarvāstivādins' *viṣayas* are defined as what is given to the five sense-organs. They fall under the heading rūpa, matter, and are therefore physical.

(b) *Sense-datum + awareness = sensation* Russell:

> Let us give the name of 'sense-data' to the things that are immediately known in sensation: such things as colours, sounds, smells, hardnesses, roughnesses, and so on. We shall give the name 'sensation' to the experience of being immediately aware of these things. Thus, whenever we see a colour, we have a sensation *of* the colour, but the colour itself is a sense-datum, not a sensation. The colour is that *of* which we are immediately aware, and the awareness itself is the sensation.[1]

In *The Relation of Sense-data to Physics*, he says, 'What the mind adds to sensibilia in fact is *merely* awareness.'[2] I shall deal with sensibilia below, but it is enough for now to mention that all sense-data are sensibilia.

The Sarvāstivāda: Sense-datum (viṣaya) + sense-organ (indriya) + awareness (vijñāna) = sensation (sparśa). Stcherbatsky gives the example: 'A moment of colour (rūpa), a moment of the sense-of-vision matter (cakṣuh), and a moment of pure consciousness (citta), arising simultaneously in close contiguity, constitute what is called a sensation (sparça) of colour.'[3] While sense-data, Russellian and Abhidharmist, are physical, sensations are for both of them mental events; (sparśa is one of the mental states (saṃskāras)).

(c) *The aware subject* Since Russellian sense-data and viṣayas are what is *given*, they must be given to something. Both Russell and the Sarvāstivāda identify the 'self', in so far as either admit its existence, with the subject *to* which sense-data/viṣayas are given. Both claim that it is at least theoretically possible to be acquainted with the subject, even though it may be impossible in practice. Russell says:

> When we try to look into ourselves we always seem to come upon some particular thought or feeling, and not upon the 'I' which has the thought or feeling. Nevertheless, there are some reasons for thinking that we are acquainted with the 'I', though the acquaintance is hard to disentangle from other things.[4]

Conze sums up the Buddhist position:

> It is easy to define 'consciousness' [vijñāna] as 'pure awareness', or discrimination (the *vi-* has the force of *dis*), but almost impossible to actually experience it in its purity. This is partly due to the extreme

difficulty of attending to an act of awareness without at the same time paying some attention also to its object.[5]

(d) *Skill needed to isolate sensations* Russell reminds us that 'the painter has to unlearn the habit of thinking that things seem to have the colour which common sense says they "really" have, and to learn the habit of seeing things as they appear.'[6] The distinction Russell is drawing is *not* simply between the ordinary man's being aware of common-sense things and the painter's being aware of sense-data. For we have seen that 'to be aware of sense-data' is 'to have sensations', and sensations are had by everyone with senses. It seems, however, that the painter does *something* different from having sensations or being aware of sense-data. If, for instance, a painter and an ordinary man (call him 'Bill') are asked how a certain table looks to them, Bill may reply, 'It looks circular, dark brown and highly polished'; and the painter, 'It looks elliptical, mostly white with uneven streaks of light brown, and with a distorted, inverted bookcase visible at one side.'

Neither of these reports need be false and there need be no disagreement between the two men. They are using the term 'looks' differently, and the two reports correspond to two uses of 'looks'. Mundle calls the painter's use '"looks"... in the phenomenological sense... or "looks$_{(ph)}$".'[7] The more everyday sense of 'estimates about objective properties of the physical things one is looking at',[8] he calls simply 'looks'. This distinction between 'looks$_{(ph)}$' and 'looks', though convenient in helping us to eliminate apparent disagreement such as that between the painter and Bill, still leaves an unanswered question. What is interesting is to discover the distinction between the kinds of looking done by the painter and by Bill which correspond to the terms 'looks$_{(ph)}$' and 'looks'. It's no good trying to deny that the painter and Bill are doing different things, because, as Russell points out, a correct report of how things look$_{(ph)}$ takes skill. This is not to say that once Bill had heard the painter's report about the table, he might not say, 'Oh, if you meant "looks" in *that* sense, you should have said so and I would have told you how it really looks (i.e. looks$_{(ph)}$).' But the point is that if the test were made, and Bill and the painter were *now* asked to say how the curtains look$_{(ph)}$, it is very likely that Bill would make mistakes. So what has the painter learned to do which Bill hasn't properly?

Disregarding differences in position and eyesight, the painter and Bill enjoy similar retinal images, are aware of similar sense-data, are having similar sensations. Yet clearly the more accurate report on these comes from the painter. Where, then, does Bill go wrong? The answer is that he is accustomed to having sensations and basing on these sensations estimates of how things 'really' are. In other words, he is accustomed to jumping immediately from noticing how things look$_{(ph)}$ to noticing how they look. But in fact he finds it difficult to notice how things look$_{(ph)}$, to pretend he is a camera, because he is unused to stopping at that. Bill does too much. Instead of reporting his sensations, he reports what *other* sensations might be had in other circumstances – viewing the curtains from a different angle etc. In practical life, that is what we need to know. You can't decide which carpet would match the curtains if you stop at one sensation of the curtains. What you need is the 'real' colour, the sensation had when viewing the curtains from certain 'typical' positions. Such a habit is this that even when Bill *tries* to report his present sensation, it is difficult for him to be objective enough. How the curtains look$_{(ph)}$ now seems too petty and accidental to be worth concentrating on; too petty and accidental to be able even to *see* properly.

This discussion brings us to the very heart of the dharma-theory, the whole point of which is, in perception, to isolate sensations, as the painter does, although perception is only a part of what is dealt with. The phenomenological skills which have to be learned by the painter are a part, though a fairly small part, of that which someone practising *smṛti* (mindfulness) has to do. While Bill's main problem was to be aware only of his sense-data, and not his estimates of a thing's objective properties, the main problem for a person practising smṛti is, as far as perception is concerned, to be aware of his sense-data and not the mass of expectations, emotional associations, evaluations and conceptual trails that occur along with them. 'He stops at what is actually seen.'[9] Bill's problem is evidently the smaller of the two, and less skill is required. The difficulties involved in 'getting dharmas into view' are acknowledged by the Abhidharmists as considerable.

(e) *A deliberately over-economical analysis* It might be imagined that if one analysed, say, a book into either Russellian sense-data or dharmas, the sense-data/dharmas could be recombined to form the book as we normally think of it. But in neither case is this true. Russell and the Abhidharmists see their metaphysical roles as involving correction of what people normally understand as the meanings of words. A book is normally understood to exist through time, independently of our sense-data. But these assumptions correspond to nothing in the new analyses. Analysis into sense-data/dharmas is not meant to be a translation of common-sense words and ideas, but an improvement on them. One might wonder where we are being led. If ordinary language as used about a book is not to be trusted, what can one trust? Why should a metaphysician's corrections of it be trusted more? One feels that in this case Ockham's razor has cut a vein, and precious meaning has been allowed to bleed away. Neither of our analysts, however, would see it like that. They would claim that some assumptions in ordinary language about common-sense objects have to be jettisoned because they are incompatible with empiricism; and most of our assumptions about a book can be shown as reasonable only *by* empiricism.

(f) *New, more real, incorrigible kind of object* Both sense-data and dharmas are held to be more real than everyday objects. The Abhidharmists say that there are only dharmas; dharmas alone are real. They are a kind of object that one does not normally realise exists because one has emotional and other vested interests in the belief in concrete, common-sense objects. The skill which we have seen to be necessary to 'get them into view' is skill, in the first place, in discovering a new kind of object. Russell says that there are 'ultimate simples out of which the world is built, and that these simples have a kind of reality not belonging to anything else.'[10]

If analysis is not simply a reduction of meanings of words to their simplest constituents, but a reduction of *things* to theirs, one inevitably arrives at this point of view. The analysis of meanings will eventually yield simple, irreducible meanings; and the reduction of things may well yield objects whose names have simple meanings. But this reduction of things, if it is not taken in the sense of discovering small physical particles (neutrons, protons etc.), can only lead to the discovery of simple realities, out of which the larger and more obvious realities are constructed.

One of the main purposes of the introduction of sense-data and dharmas is to achieve certainty. Even though we need skill to isolate them, we are, when we have done so, acquainted with something whose real existence we cannot doubt. This is not held to be merely the kind of incorrigibility made possible by talking of 'how objects appear'. We can be certain of the truth of statements about the reality of sense-data and dharmas *not* because we preface them with 'It seems to me that . . .', but because we have found the atoms of our experience, the particulars with which we are directly acquainted and cannot, therefore, be mistaken about.

To regard sense-data (and mental states) and dharmas as incorrigible not *despite* their privacy but rather *because* of it, proved to be one of the places where the weaknesses of the theory showed up most clearly. In the next chapter I shall show how this happened.

(g) *Momentary* Part of the reason why skill is necessary to isolate one's awareness of (Russellian) sense-data is that they are momentary.

> There had been a metaphysical prejudice always that if a thing is really real, it has to last either forever or for a fairly decent length of time. That to my mind is an entire mistake. The things that are really real last a very short time. Again I am not denying that there *may* be things that last forever, or for thousands of years; I only say

> that those are not within our experience, and that the real things that we know by experience last for a very short time, one tenth or half a second, or whatever it may be.[11]

All dharmas (except space and Nirvāṇa) are momentary. The Sarvāstivādins reckon their duration as theoretically measurable, though extremely short.[12] So basic to Buddhism is this idea of momentariness that it is included in the well-known 'three marks' (lakṣana) of conditioned dharmas. All dharmas are *adverse* or painful (duhkha) as compared with the Unconditioned (Nirvāṇa); *not-self* (anātman) – generally taken to mean void of substance when applied to inanimate objects; and *impermanent* (anitya). 'Impermanence' or 'momentariness' in Buddhist writings always has a built-in negative evaluation; and is indeed made explicit: 'What is impermanent is not worth rejoicing over nor worth approval nor worth cleaving to.'[13] This expresses conditioned dharmas' distasteful lack of stability as contrasted with Nirvāṇa. Of course, there is no parallel with Russell on this last point.

(h) *Momentariness not quite satisfactory* Neither Russell nor the Sarvāstivādins, however, could quite bring themselves to accept the restriction of the life of particulars to the present moment, and they found themselves drawn to a compromise position somewhere between momentariness and common-sense realism. Neither of their compromise theories found much favour with the analysts who were their respective contemporaries. Of course, compromises are not very philosophically satisfying.

Russell's compromise was to introduce sensibilia.

> I shall give the name *sensibilia* to those objects which have the same metaphysical and physical status as sense-data without necessarily being data to any mind. Thus the relation of a *sensibile* to a sense-datum is like that of a man to a husband: a man becomes a husband by entering into the relation of marriage, and similarly a sensibile becomes a sense-datum by entering into the relation of acquaintance. It is important to have both terms; for we wish to discuss whether an object which is at one time a sense-datum can still exist at a time when it is not a sense-datum.[14]

This theory has the apparent advantage that it makes the simple particulars out of which the universe is constructed neither private nor momentary. The existence of the book you are reading will no longer be dubious when the book is unperceived. The gaps between sense-data are filled with sensibilia. The sensibilia can enter into the relation of acquaintance with anyone and so the book, though still a construction from more real simple items, is in a sense public. Are sensibilia a new type of entity? Some have thought not. Mundle, for instance, argues that the introduction of sensibilia 'conforms with Occam's Razor, for we are not postulating a new type of entity, but are merely attributing continuous existence to entities of which we are immediately aware [sc. sense-data].'[15] Yet this cannot be right. Sense-data were defined in terms of being sensed, and so we are necessarily aware of them, but sensibilia need not be sensed. So sensibilia cannot be simply enduring sense-data. A sense-datum with 'continuous existence' would be that of which one was aware in a drawn-out sensation of an unchanging quality. That would make sense-data other than momentary, though at the cost of ruling out all continued visual sensations except those requiring manic stares, but it would not make sense-data public.

The Sarvāstivādins' compromise was the 'three times' theory. This was the main peculiarity of the Sarvāstivāda as a school. Their name is derived from the view that 'everything exists' (sarva asti) – that dharmas exist not only in the present but in some sense also in the past and future. All conditioned dharmas (not only sense-data (viṣayas), but of course including those) exist through all 'three times'. To someone watching the 'rise and fall' of dharmas, they simply appear and then disappear. The Sarvāstivādins, while agreeing with this last point, add that dharmas 'move' from the future to the present, when one is aware of them, and then to the past, when awareness of them ceases. But they exist at all three times, not only in the present. A dharma's own-being, Stcherbatsky tells us, 'exists always, in past, present and future. It is not eternal (nitya), because eternality means absence of change, but it represents the potential appearances of the element [dharma] into phenomenal existence, and its past appearances as well.'[16]

Although Russell and the Sarvāstivādins added 'potential appearances' to 'appearances', their reasons were different. Briefly, Russell's reason was that the common-sense things which could be reconstructed from sense-data did not exist continuously because they were sometimes unsensed. Things reconstructed from sensibilia did, however, exist continuously. The Sarvāstivādins' reason was that causality, memory and permanent character changes[17] are incomprehensible if nothing outside the present moment is real. But in both cases there was the feeling that in moving from common-sense things to momentary particulars, too much in the way of permanence had been lost. Ockham's Razor had indeed cut too deep; and these sticking-plaster theories were the result. We end up with particulars, once defined as sense-given and momentary, as what we are acquainted with here and now, whose existence is yet extended out of the here and now. And the extension is in order that we can predicate of our particulars some of the attributes of common-sense things which seem resistant to reduction to momentary simples.

(i) *Vision the paradigm case* The basic evidence here is so overwhelming that it seems hardly worth setting it out. On the Buddhist side, Jayatilleke has shown that 'the emphasis that "knowing" (jñānaṃ) must be based on "seeing" (passaṃ) or direct perceptive experience, makes Buddhism a form of Empiricism.'[18] 'The central truths of Buddhism are "seen". One "comprehends the Noble Truths and sees them" ... Even Nirvāṇa is "seen".'[19] There are in fact various visual similes for the different ways of seeing Nirvāṇa. Seeing it for the first time at the 'supramundane' stage of the path is like 'seeing a king' in the sense of setting eyes on him; but attaining Nirvāṇa is like seeing a king in the sense of 'seeing the king on some particular business',[20] i.e. meeting him and getting to know him. Not only unconditioned dharmas are 'seen'. One has to 'get dharmas into view', 'watch their rise and fall'; ignorance 'covers the dharmas from our sight', while wisdom (prajñā) 'abolishes the darkness of delusion which conceals the own-being of dharmas.'[21]

Equally important, in very nearly every case where perception is discussed in Hīnayāna works, the example given, where one is necessary, is one of vision. Admittedly, in the usual list of the five senses, vision comes before hearing, smelling, tasting and touching, so one might think it was just a matter of vision being the first to hand. But notice that visual sense-data are *rūpa-viṣaya*, even though all five senses fall under the heading of matter (rūpa). It certainly looks as if vision was taken to be perception par excellence.

In Russell's case, one might sometimes forget that there are sense-data other than visual ones. The others are mentioned only, or very nearly only, when sense-data are being defined, but are afterwards ignored. Not that this is peculiar to him: to regard vision as the 'standard case' of perception is normal for the vast majority of philosophers of perception both Indian and European. This may be partly because our languages are full of visual similes for knowing, but I think there is a more straightforward reason. Vision is the only sense which is likely to suggest the need for a term like 'sense-datum'. The table has the properties of roundness and brownness but not also those of ellipticality and whiteness. Yet we know, it seems, that something has the latter properties because we can see them, and so need a name to refer to this 'something'. This is quite understandable in the case of vision, but when we come to consider the other four senses, a name like 'sense-datum', though it can be applied, does not seem to mark one side of an important distinction.

To say, 'I have a white, elliptical sense-datum' is roughly equivalent to 'the table looks$_{(ph)}$ white and elliptical to me', and one can see that these statements are contrasted with 'the table looks brown and round to me.' But if we now consider taste and smell, we may say, 'I have sweet-tasting and rose-scented sense-data', which is roughly equivalent to 'the plum tastes$_{(ph)}$ sweet and the flower smells$_{(ph)}$ like a rose.' With what, however, are *these* contrasted? In the case of normal perception, nothing at all. This was not the case with vision. The table does *not* normally look$_{(ph)}$ brown and round. Normal vision allows a distinction between 'looks' and 'looks$_{(ph)}$'; with normal smell and taste, there are no equivalent distinctions.

With hearing, sense-datum language may seem a little more useful, for we may wish to mark off the sound as it really is from the sound as I hear it. Unfortunately, it is just as before. Talking of taste and smell sense-data represents virtually no advance on talking of tasting and smelling, and the same is true of hearing. We *do* distinguish between our estimate of the 'objective properties' of a sound and how it sounds to us. But we cannot distinguish how it sounds from how it sounds$_{(ph)}$. Suppose the two of us are a mile and a half from a church in which a bell is being rung. I say:

> 'How does the noise of the bell sound to you?'
> 'Faint and intermittent.'
> 'Doesn't it, in another sense of "sound" (i.e. not "sound$_{(ph)}$") sound loud and regular?'
> 'In *no* sense does it sound loud and regular to me. It might to somebody near the church, but that is another matter.'

That is, to observe merely our sense-data requires some effort in the case of vision, but with taste, smell and hearing all we have to do is notice how, in the most obvious sense, things taste, smell and sound. So far as I can tell, the same is true also of the sense of touch. Tactile sense-data are usually just 'how things feel'. I have left touching till last, however, because there *are* a set of cases in which 'feeling$_{(ph)}$' is distinguished within our normal experience from 'feeling'. Suppose that round table which I have mentioned irritatingly often to have metal brackets underneath to stop the legs falling off. If I know both that the room where the table is has been at a constant temperature for a long time, *and* the elementary facts about conduction of heat in solids, I will know that brackets and legs are at the same temperature. Most likely, the brackets will *feel*$_{(ph)}$ colder than the legs, but I can interpret this as compatible with what may be, for me, the fact that brackets and legs *feel* as if they were equally warm. Only in rather special cases like this can a thing feel$_{(ph)}$ one way and feel another. The case is special because many people are hazy about the conduction of heat in solids, and 'tactile sense-datum' will be a useful phrase only for those who bear it in mind when they touch the brackets and legs or whatever. For the others, tactile sense-datum statements could be as well replaced by 'how things feel' statements.

Of course there is no *logical* difficulty in extending the use of 'sense-data/viṣaya' to the non-visual senses, even though it may seem to express one side of a distinction which has no other side. Russell and the Abhidharmists would have wanted to keep non-visual sense-data/viṣayas, not simply for reasons of consistency but because they both wanted to get away from talking about 'things'. Even though statements about how things taste, for example, are normally complete translations of statements about taste sense-data, 'things' did not really exist in Russellian and Abhidarmist metaphysics. As we know, they were replaced by particulars taken from our analysed experience, and some of the particulars were meant to be sense-data in the 'new kind of object' sense of the term. But sense-data as a new kind of object, it now turns out, are only really applicable to vision (if indeed they are defensible at all). The quick proof of this is that it does take skill to isolate visual sensations, but no skill to isolate non-visual ones. The Buddhists, admittedly, can point to the skill needed to separate them from attendant emotions etc. but in purely perceptual terms, no skill is needed.

Mental States

We are aware, Russell tells us,[22] of sense-data in perception and of our mental states in introspection. These include being aware of feeling pleasure or pain, desiring or wishing for something and all our thoughts. Such states are only objects of acquaintance when we become aware of them. The fact that I desire food does not necessarily mean that I am aware of my desire for food; but there is a mental state which can be called 'my desiring food' of which I *can* become aware. It seems unlikely, in this example of Russell's, that I would fail to be aware of the mental state, but Russell's account does leave open the possibility of mental states which I may, not merely logically, but in practical likelihood, overlook.

To introspect Russellian mental states, then, requires skill, even if it is sometimes a rather easily acquired skill. What this tells us is that 'mental states' are to be thought of as new kinds of objects rather than as something more obvious. 'My desiring food' is not simply a translation of 'the fact that I desire food'. In Russell's words, ' "my desiring food" is an object with which I am acquainted.'[23] Mental states are objects, real particulars, every bit as much as are sense-data. It begins to look as if visual experience has been taken as a model not only for non-visual senses, but for non-sensual states too.

The Abhidharmists set out their attitude to these non-sensual data in a rather more blatant way than did Russell. They made what Russell called 'introspection' a sixth sense, or at least a 'receptive faculty' on the same standing as the five senses. The *āyatana* division is common to all early schools, and is a classification of all the 'entrance doors' (āyatanas) through which data are received. There are twelve: sight organ and visual sense-data; hearing organ and aural sense-data; organ of smell and smell sense-data; taste organ and taste sense-data; tactile organ and tactile sense-data; mental organ (*manas* = mind) and mental data. It may be thought surprising that Buddhists, who have always been keen to reject any kind of substantial ego as a dread heresy, should have kept throughout their history to a distinction between the receiving mind and its mental contents (i.e. between *citta* and *caitta*). And even though the receiving mind (manas, citta) is, naturally, nothing that one can 'receive' – that is, it is contentless – it is held on to by Buddhists because they cannot do without it. They need it for the same reason as Russell does. Vision is a relation between visual sense-data and the visual organ. There are objects 'out there' which 'come in' by a certain route. Being aware of states like hatred, envy or tranquillity is, in a similar way, a relation between mental data and the 'mental organ'. The objects are 'in here' but are not in quite far enough. When we are *aware* of these objects with the 'mental organ' they are *properly* in. Russell called the awareness of sense-data 'sensation', but never seemed to feel the need of an equivalent term for mental states. Let us call them 'mentations'. Right; sense-data are not mental, but are situated only a small distance outside the mind, where we may be unaware of them. When we *become* aware of them, they come right into the mind, and this awareness is a sensation. Mental states *are* inside the mind to start with, although we may still be unaware of them. When we become aware of them, they come into the mind in a somehow deeper way and this awareness is a mentation.

This could serve as a model for either Russell's views on the mind or those of the Abhidarmists. But neither were really happy about regarding the aware subject as an entity. Russell expresses doubts about it in *The Problems of Philosophy*, and not long afterwards comes to reject the self and, therefore, the distinction between sense-data and sensations (and between mental states and 'mentations'). The Abhidharmists are always keen to point out that citta (consciousness) is simply 'one's being aware of this, then this...' Just the same, as long as Russell believed in sense-data and mental facts as objects he needed a subject for them to be related to. And as long as the Abhidharmists took their experiential dharmas as data which could be 'got into view' in the practice of mindfulness (smṛti), they could never wholly avoid reifying consciousness as that which gets dharmas into view.

The Abhidharmists' 'mental objects' (caitta) comprise feelings (vedanā), which I dealt with above;[24] saṃjña;[25] and the saṃskāras. Apart from the 'neither-physical-nor-mental samskāras' of the Sarvāstivādins, which, as we saw, can be regarded as relations, the saṃskāras are meant to be all the separately identifiable mental states there can be. Physical things like boots and buns are what Russell would call logical fictions, constructions out of elementary data. According to the Abhidharmists, they are constructions not only from sense-data but also from the emotional reactions they 'cause' and from various other attendant mental states. That is not to say that mind and matter are not clearly separated by the Abhidharmists. They would argue that being aware of the dharmas 'comprising' a boot enables one to separate sense-data from the purely mental states accompanying them. Commonsense too supposes that the physical thing, the boot, is quite separate from our thoughts and feelings about it. The difference is that, for the Buddhists, mind and matter, though still separated, come a good deal closer than common-sense admits. Like Russell's sense-data, the Abhidharmists' viṣayas are not mental, but come awfully close to it. And the Abhidharmists, unlike Russell, stress the subtle 'co-operation' between sense-data and mental states. Our sense-data serve as conditions for our mental states, which in turn affect our sense-data. For Russell, there are five senses telling one about what is outside one's mind, and introspection, an 'inner sense', telling one about what is inside it.

But apart from links with perception, the Abhidharmists' 'caittas' (mental states) are also what one introspects. They are the basic ingredients of all of one's mental life. What is astonishing is that there are only, for the Sarvāstivāda, 46 mental states. Feelings and saṃjña count as only one dharma each and we obviously cannot count the neither-physical-*nor-mental* saṃskāras. The reason there are so few is that the analysis of mental experiences is made for a purpose, and the list of basic mental particulars must contain only items to which it is worth paying attention for the achievement of the purpose. The purpose is, of course, the attainment of Nirvāṇa, the most important of all the dharmas. And we must not forget that skill is needed to isolate mental particulars. It would be a large mistake to equate the saṃskāras, the feelings and saṃjña with my mental states as they appear to me at 'first glance'. A similar distinction to that between 'looks' and 'looks$_{(ph)}$' applies here too. It is better in a way to compare them with the elements of modern physics, of which about a hundred are sufficient to combine to form the world in all its variety.

Unconditioned Dharmas

Seventy-two of the Sarvāstivādins' 75 dharmas are conditioned (saṃskṛta). Their appearance and disappearance, or 'passage through the three times' as the Sarvāstivādins would prefer, are conditioned by other conditioned dharmas. The whole world as experienced by us is a set of conditioned dharmas of 72 kinds. All conditioned dharmas are momentary and we are told that there is no satisfaction to be gained in relying on them.

Unconditioned (asaṃskṛta) dharmas, on the other hand, are those which cannot be conditioned or brought about by anything and which cannot be a condition for anything else. The Sarvāstivāda count three of them. There is space (ākāśa) and two varieties of Nirvāṇa. I do not want to discuss Nirvāṇa at length because such a lot has already been said by others. What is of interest, though, for our present purposes is whether Nirvāṇa is a particular or a quality.

If it is a *particular*, we can think of it as in some ways akin to a spatial heaven. The Jehovah's Witnesses' idea of heaven, for instance, is an idea of a place, presumably with boundaries, which remains a single heaven even though it is a heaven for many different people. They share it rather as people might share a room. In suggesting this simile, I do not suggest that Nirvāṇa might be a physical heaven, but that it might be something which people share, or even 'partake of' because there is only one Nirvāṇa (or two for the Sarvāstivāda). If it is a *quality*, we can think of it as akin to the conditioned dharmas in that there will be particular instances of Nirvāṇa, each identifiable by being particulars of the 'Nirvāṇic type'. To say that Nirvāṇa might be an experiential dharma is to say that it might be a quality common to experiences of 'mine', 'yours', etc. I put 'mine' and 'yours' in scare quotes because when Nirvāṇa is attained, it is realised finally that 'non-self' (anātman) applies to oneself. And if I am not really my-self in the way I imagine I am, it may be that to talk about whether or not Nirvāṇa can be one of my experiences is a mistake.

That is also the reason why warnings should be issued about calling the two possible interpretations of Nirvāṇa, 'objective world' and 'subjective state'. These are the phrases used by Johansson[26] in his discussion of the Theravāda concept of Nirvāṇa. But since one *can* translate the problem into a logical one about whether 'Nirvāṇa' names a particular or a quality, these difficulties about 'non-self' need not worry us too much.

Johansson's conclusion about Nirvāṇa is that it is a transformation of personality and consciousness which the Abhidharmists falsified into an objective, independent reality. He bases this largely on a discussion of the Therāvada text, 'Udāna', which contains the famous passage: 'Monks, there is an unborn, a not-become, a not-made, a not-compounded... If there were not, there would be apparent no escape from this here that is born, become, made, compounded.'[27] According to Johansson, the Abhidharmists took statements like 'there is an unborn' in the above and similar passages to be claims about an entity. But it is, he suggests, more likely to be a reference to the fact that an Arhat (one who has attained Nirvāṇa) is not reborn. 'There is...' does not mean 'there is an entity (a particular) which is unborn...', but rather, 'there is that condition of a person in which he is not reborn...'

There are, he admits, some passages which suggest that everyone attains the *same* Nirvāṇa in some sense. In Udāna 55, for instance, Nirvāṇa is compared with an ocean which never shrinks or overflows no matter how many rivers flow into it. No matter how many monks pass finally away into Nirvāṇa, no shrinkage or overflow occurs. But on the whole Johansson is inclined to the view that Nirvāṇa is a subjective state. He points out, as contributory evidence, that there are objective 'worlds' attained by the successive stages of trance (dhyāna), objective enough to reborn in, and quite separate from *this* world; but even the highest trance is distinct from Nirvāṇa itself.

Turning now from the Theravāda to the Sarvāstivāda, we find not one Nirvāṇa-dharma, but two. One is the cessation (nirodha) of conditioned dharmas led up to by efforts to achieve wisdom (prajñā). If one 'gets the dharmas into view' sufficiently well, they stop continually pestering one. That this is at the very least not nonsense can be confirmed by anyone. One has only to objectively watch one's mental processes, identifying with them as little as possible, to find that they calm down after a few minutes. Soon, however, one again becomes greedy for mental thrills and begins to cheat, 'secretly' siding with some mental processes and not others.

But to return from unscholarly evangelism to the second kind of Nirvāṇa: we turn from 'cessation by discriminative knowledge' (pratisaṃkhyā-nirodha) to cessation without discriminative knowledge. Here the way to Nirvāṇa is not by wisdom but by the expiring both of the impurities which lead to rebirth and of the arising of further impure dharmas. I do not see how these two kinds of cessation can be anything other than 'subjective states'. The alternatives are to posit either two 'objective worlds', one for each of the two kinds of cessation, or one objective world – Nirvāṇa – reachable in two ways. The latter can be ruled out completely as not what the Sarvāstivādins meant – why did they not mention such a world? And the former clashes with the frequent statements that cessation (nirodha) is, for those concerned, a permanent achievement or possession (prāpti). The 'stream' (santāna), a euphemism for 'individual', includes dharmas as 'its own' by courtesy of 'possession', one of the relation-dharmas. Since cessation too can be possessed, it is evidently a subjective state.

It looks, then, as if even though there are certain traditions about Nirvāṇa as akin to a place, it can be interpreted more easily as a quality common to events in different people's lives. Even space, the other unconditioned dharma, is more of an experiential dharma than one might imagine. The term 'space' (ākāśa) is often used to refer to spaces I can experience, gaps between things. It never bears much relation to Newtonian space. Guenther refers to the space of the Sarvāstivādins as 'the oriented space of an individual's life-world.'[28] Giving the Theravāda view of space, Buddhaghosa says, 'Space has the mark (lakṣana) of delimiting matter. Its function is to display the boundaries of matter. It is manifested . . . as an untouchedness, as the state of gaps and apertures.'[29] The Theravāda, however, did not regard space as unconditioned.

Even though Nirvāṇa and space seem sometimes to be thought of as big particulars (so that my enlightenment is part of the same Nirvāṇa as is yours, and the space I occupy is part of the one big space) it seems more consistent to think of them as primarily experiential. Leaving space out of account for now, we can offer some confirmation of Johansson's thesis from a different direction. It is *possible* that although the names for conditioned dharmas have to serve as names for qualities of many particulars, the names for conditioned dharmas are more like proper names. (Even giving Nirvāṇa a capital letter seems to make it resemble a spatial heaven!) But the burden of proof lies with anyone who suggests that names of unconditioned dharmas refer to unique particulars, while those for conditioned dharmas do not.

Naturally we can find no parallel with unconditioned dharmas in Russell's writings. The point I want to stress, however, is that even on this topic, where the Sarvāstivādins are at the greatest distance from Russell, there is no good reason for thinking that when they came to consider the Unconditioned, they formulated new policies about the logic of names for particulars and qualities, or about the turning of everything into objects. Even an experience so apparently unsuitable for reification, the central experience of Buddhist spirituality, is made into an existing object which one can 'see'.

Part Two

WITTGENSTEIN AND THE MAHĀYĀNA

3 Sensations and Language

The Basic Criticism

According to the analysts every word has a simple object for its meaning. But the way we actually use a word like 'hope', for example, often tends to cloud its meaning, so we have to dig deep for it. If we analyse all cases of hoping, we will eventually discover what they all have in common. This common element is what the word 'hope' *really* means; it is the essence of hope. And we can if we are careful *experience* essences. We can as it were *see* the meaning, the object, the essence, so that no doubt can remain.

To watch dharmas come and go, to be acquainted with particulars and their properties, were claimed by the Abhidharmists and Russell respectively to be possible. If we analyse our sense-experience and our understanding of terms for relations etc. into their ultimate constituents, we actually *meet* these essences. In some cases, such as that of relations, this claim had been less than straightforwardly acceptable. But in a case like hope, what could be clearer? If I am hoping, I *know* that I am. I can't be sure whether anybody else is, because I can't look inside them. In my own case, however, there is an inner state which is real, here, indubitable.

Now, to deny both that words necessarily correspond to objects and that there are essences which we can experience for ourselves seems, on the face of it, something of a relief when we consider relations. But when applied to 'hope' (and many other things), it involves what must appear as an unacceptable gap in my inner life. 'What! no inner states? I'm not dead inside!' It is of great importance to realise that the denial of 'objects and essences' does not result in a hideous pumping out of inner experience. What should happen, if the advice of the analysts' critics is taken, is that our inner experience is no longer interpreted in terms of private, simple objects.

The trouble is, according to Wittgenstein, that 'if we construe the grammar of the expression of sensation on the model of "object and designation", the object drops out of consideration as irrelevant.'[1] If hope[2] is something essentially private, there is no reason to think that we all use the word to refer to the same kind of object and so no knowing which, if any, of us is using the word in the 'correct' way. Nor is there even reason to think that *I* always use the word correctly[3] (now = 'consistently'), because, since there is no way of checking, the distinction between 'true consistency' and 'inconsistency which I took to be consistency' vanishes. It makes no difference, on the 'naming the inner object' hypothesis, *what* the inner object is.

The Mahāyāna was also keen to escape from the idea of privately nameable inner objects. 'Getting the dharmas into view' had been for the Abhidharmists the prime virtue, and was known as *prajñā* (wisdom). But there sprang up a host of Mahāyāna works in which the prajñā of viewing dharmas is left behind and is replaced by *Prajñāpāramitā*, the 'wisdom which has gone beyond' or 'the perfection of wisdom'. To gain this perfect wisdom involves realising not only that the dharmas are objects implying an inner, unreachable self just as much as the 'objects in the external world' they were meant to do away with, but also that, as with Wittgenstein, there is no way of 'correctly' identifying and naming necessarily private dharmas. 'Haribhadra explains that one "cannot distinguish the various objects to which the different words refer".'[4] The Hīnayāna had held that common-sense objects were logical fictions; there were only dharmas. But 'the Mahāyāna now adds that these [dharmas] are "empty of self" in the sense that each one is nothing in and by itself, and is therefore indistinguishable from any other any dharma and so ultimately non-existent.'[5]

All dharmas, according to the Abhidharmists, could be identified by their distinguishing or defining features – their 'marks'; but it turns out that the marks do not afford any identification after all. The Prajñāpāramitā says repeatedly: 'Dharmas are without marks, with one mark only, that is, no mark.'[6] The object has 'dropped out' and, as with Wittgenstein, we are left with a name referring *apparently* to nothing: '*Subhuti*: It is wonderful to see the extent to which the Tathāgata has demonstrated the true nature of all these dharmas, and yet one cannot properly talk about the true nature of all these dharmas (in the sense of predicating distinctive attributes to separate real entities).'[7] 'Words . . . express dharmas through adventitious designations which are imagined and unreal. A Bodhisattva who courses in perfect wisdom does not review any reality behind those words, and, in consequence, does not settle down in them.'[8] 'All dharmas lie outside conventional expression and discourse . . . it is not they that have been conventionally expressed or uttered.'[9]

The stumbling-block, then, had been the assumption that words imply objects 'behind' them:

> If you say he sees a private picture before him, which he is describing, you have still made an assumption about what he has before him. And that means that you can describe it or do describe it more closely. If you admit that you haven't any notion what kind of thing

it might be that he has before him – then what leads you into saying, in spite of that, that he has something before him? Isn't it as if I were to say of someone: 'He *has* something. But I don't know whether it is money, or debts, or an empty till.'[10]

The plausibility of 'private sensations' depends on imagining that the structure of our 'inner life' resembles the structure of the way we talk about it: 'According to ultimate reality, no distinction or difference can be apprehended between these dharmas. The Tathāgata has described them as talk.'[11] 'When we look into ourselves as we do philosophy, we often get to see just such a picture. A full-blown pictorial representation of our grammar. Not facts; but as it were illustrated turns of speech.'[12]

That it was a mistake to construe the grammar of the expression of dharmas on the model of 'object and designation' was also expressed by saying that all dharmas were *empty* (śūnya). Emptiness (śūnyatā) is the central concept of the Mādhyamika school (founded by Nāgārjuna, 2nd century A.D.), which absorbed and sharpened the ideas in the Prajñāpāramitā works. To say that 'all dharmas are empty' is not simply to say that 'there are no dharmas.' It is to reject the assumption that one can analyse the world into simple, existent particulars (dharmas with 'own-being). They are only 'illustrated turns of speech.'

'That an entity is empty means that own-being is absent from it. When the entities are pieces of language, it means that they are symbols empty of object-content.'[13]

At this point, it is easy to make a mistake. If private sensations/dharmas are only 'illustrated turns of speech'/'symbols empty of object-content', the word 'hope', for instance, doesn't refer to anything. There is no hope after all; only a word. Naturally, one becomes impatient at this, because hope is obviously a lot more than a word. In fact, both Wittgenstein and the Mādhyamika have been accused of substituting a gap for our inner life. But neither did. Wittgenstein says,

> 'And yet you again and again reach the conclusion that the sensation itself is a *nothing*' – Not at all. It is not a *something*, but not a *nothing* either! The conclusion was only that a nothing would serve just as well as a something about which nothing could be said. We have only rejected the grammar which tries to force itself on us here.[14]

The Mādhyamikas are also careful to point out that dharmas are neither somethings nor nothings, neither exist nor don't: 'The Lord: Someone who has set out in the Bodhisattva-vehicle should know, see and resolve upon all dharmas in such a way that he has nothing to do with either the notion of a dharma or the notion of a no-dharma.'[15]

The Mādhyamika reject the Abhidharmists' interpretation of the 'Middle Way' of the Buddha as an avoidance of the doctrines of permanently abiding substance (Eternalism) on the one hand and that of the impossibility of continuity (Nihilism) on the other. Instead, they interpret it as neither affirming nor denying the existence of dharmas. If they had denied the existence of dharmas outright, they would have been nihilists, a claim they reject.[16]

This caution about nihilism is nicely exemplified in a Mahāyāna reinterpretation of the famous Raft parable. The Buddha's teaching is compared to a Raft, which successfully transports people to the 'other shore' (Nirvāṇa), but which is of no more use when the goal is attained. The interesting sentence in the parable occurs at the end. 'You, monks, by understanding the Parable of the Raft, should get rid even of (right) mental objects, all the more of wrong ones.'[17] Now, the words translated as 'right' and 'wrong' mental objects are *dharma* and *adharma* respectively. The Hīnayāna could do no other than interpret the statement in the way just shown, as pointing out the 'beyond good and evil' character of Nirvāṇa. The Mahāyāna, however, use it in this way: 'A Bodhisattva should therefore certainly not take up a dharma nor a non-dharma. Therefore this saying has been taught by the Tathāgata in a hidden sense: "Those who know the discourse on dharma as a raft should forsake dharmas, and how much more so non-dharmas." '[18]

So the private object, for both Wittgenstein and the Mahāyāna, drops out of consideration as irrelevant, leaving a name which doesn't refer to anything. Nothing can really be said about it, yet we have seen that there are cautions against leaving matters as crude as that. In so far as the private object is a *something*, or at least 'not a nothing', what *can* be said about it (even if it is only abuse!)? Only that it is logically isolated. The private sensation is high and dry; the tide of 'reidentification of particulars' cannot reach it. 'We as it were turned a knob which looked as if it could be used to turn some part of the machine; but it was a mere ornament, not connected with the mechanism at all.'[19] 'A wheel that can be turned though nothing else moves with it, is not part of the mechanism.'[20]

Similarly, for the Prajñāpāramitā, each dharma is isolated (vivikta), because it is unrelated to everything else. 'He should cognize all dharmas, form etc. as empty in their essential original nature; he should cognize them as isolated in their own-being.'[21] Conze says, 'A dharma is called "empty" when one considers that it has no properties, "isolated" when one considers that it has no relations to other dharmas.'[22] As with Wittgenstein's similes, to call dharmas 'isolated' is not just a way of saying that each private object is 'separate' from the rest of the world. Wittgenstein's similes tell us that being separate in *that* way is to be something which is of no use to us; which amounts to nothing when we try to make use of the idea of it. And in just the same way, the Mahāyāna takes 'isolated' to amount to the same as 'empty'. What has being isolated got to do with being empty? Well, we have names for sensation/dharmas. But what the names refer to makes no difference. So on the one hand we can say that sensation-words/dharma-words are left referring to logically isolated objects (a wheel not part of the mechanism/dharmas which are vivikta); or on the other we can say that there is no identifiable object which is the sensation/dharma (the object drops out of consideration ... a nothing would serve just as well / dharmas are empty of their own-being, are nothing in themselves).

All very nice, you might say, but nothing has really been said yet. A certain philosophical position on private sensations has been shown as unstable and accordingly rejected. But what is supposed to replace it? The answer to this comes from two directions. We can try to understand how *words* function if they no longer derive their meaning from objects to which they refer. And we can try to understand what view of our '*inner life*' we ought to have now that the private object, experiencing essences, view is jettisoned. It is obvious that from the Mahāyāna–Wittgenstein point of view, words and 'inner experiences' can and must be considered separately in a way in which they had not been before, because they are no longer bound together with a one-one correlation.

Words

The doctrine that there were two levels of understanding, one shallow, conventional and more or less false, the other deep, absolute and true, had been taught in various forms in Hīnayāna schools. It came into its own, however, with the Mādhyamika, who formulated it as the theory of the 'Two Truths'. 'Worldly, conventional, or expressional truth [saṃvṛti-satya] means language and verbal thought. The absolute truth [paramārtha-satya] is said to be inexpressible and inconceivable.'[23] Conventional truth cannot, of course, be validly expressed in statements referring to private objects, essences etc. since all experiences 'are only figured but not represented by discursive symbols. Once this is granted, the functional value of language is admitted by the Mādhyamika.'[24]

This functional view of language means that, for the Mādhyamikas, statements of conventional truth can be used to help one understand absolute truth, even though they cannot refer to or correspond to matters of absolute truth. 'Without reliance on conventional truth, the absolute truth is not taught.'[25] Streng points out that, for Nāgārjuna as well as for Wittgenstein, 'words and expression-patterns are simply practical tools of human life, which *in themselves* do not carry intrinsic meaning and do not necessarily have meaning by referring to something outside the language system.'[26]

Wittgenstein is perhaps best known for his insistence that words derive meaning not from their referents but from their *use*. 'Let the use of words teach you their meaning.'[27] 'Language is an instrument. Its concepts are instruments.'[28] 'Now what do the words of this language *signify*? – What is supposed to shew what they signify, if not the kind of use they have?'[29]

It is when we forget that language is a set of tools of various kinds that the paradox about private sensations appears. The paradox is that sensations are not *nothing* because there is a difference between, for example, pain behaviour with and without pain; and are not *something* because nothing can be said about the in principle unidentifiable sensation. But, 'the paradox disappears only if we make a radical break with the idea that language always functions in one way, always serves the same purpose; to convey thoughts – which may be about houses, pains, good and evil, or anything else you please.'[30]

The meanings of words are not, for Wittgenstein, discoverable by finding the label on which a word is written and following the string to the object. We discover them by plotting the uses we make of them; by tracing the way a word can fit in to the propositions of a given language-game:

> The mistake we are liable to make could be expressed thus: We are looking for the use of a sign, but we look for it as though it were an object *co-existing* with the sign. (One of the reasons for this mistake is again that we are looking for a 'thing corresponding to a substantive.')[31]

Nāgārjuna pointed out the same mistake:

> These stanzas [of Nāgārjuna's] refute the contention that since the Dharma talks about the passions (kleśas) and misconceptions (viparyāsas), these must be existent. This contention is a typical example of the 'doctrine of names'..., the belief that words must mean something and thus that if there is a word, there must be a thing as its counterpart. Nāgārjuna denies this.[32]

'Pain', for instance, does not simply mean the object called 'pain'. It means, amongst other ways of putting it, 'the difference between pain behaviour with and without pain.' The apparent circularity of this does not matter, because it cannot be avoided. This is partly for the obvious reason that one cannot very well show how a word is used without using the word; and partly because the only alternative is to try to stick the word 'pain' directly on to a pain –

> But what is it like to give a sensation a name? Say it is pronouncing the name while one has the sensation and possibly concentrating on the sensation – but what of it? Does this name thereby get magic powers? And why on earth do I call these sounds the 'name' of a sensation? I know what I do with the name of a man or of a number, but have I by this act of 'definition' given the name a use?[33]

If we try to define a word, we keep coming back to the facts about how people use language. The distinctions between the meanings of different words point not to different objects which are necessarily distinct but to the fact that people have come to draw certain distinctions. Pears says of Wittgenstein on this matter,

> It is true that everything is what it is and not another thing, but this only means that there are indefinitely many distinctions which could be drawn in language... our desire for an objective backing [for necessity], however natural it may be, can never be satisfied. The only relevant facts are facts about our linguistic practices.[34]

For Nāgārjuna, the distinctions drawn between dharmas are also based not on objective fact but on the distinguishing which is done by people: 'Space does not exist at all before its mark (lakṣana). If it would exist before its mark, then one must falsely conclude that there would be something without a mark.'[35] And in a Prajñāpāramitā sutra: 'A man may speak of space by way of definite definition, but of space no definite definition exists;... space is conventionally expressed, but is not conventionally expressed by way of defining or accomplishing any dharma whatever.'[36]

It isn't just that we can divide up the objects in the world in any way we choose. We divide up the world *into* 'objects'. Once we have made the distinctions, the distinctions are real enough, but nothing new has been brought into existence, the world has changed in no way except the way in which we use words. Even here we must be careful not to slip back into the assumption of 'essences'. It is not that when a distinction has been made we can *then* (at last!) compare the word with the object we have made it represent. There *are no* essences for the words to represent.

Inner Life

Why doesn't Wittgenstein tell us what is to replace private sensations? The answer is that he can't, because if we try to find words to *corre-*

spond to what goes on when we hope, have pain, etc., we are forced by a misleading grammar into positing inner objects. Wittgenstein isn't denying that we hope and so on: 'We have only rejected the grammar which tries to force itself on us here.'[37] 'If I do speak of a fiction, then it is of a *grammatical* fiction.'[38]

> 'But surely you cannot deny that, for example, in remembering, an inner process takes place.' What gives the impression that we want to deny anything? When one says 'Still, an inner process does take place here' – one wants to go on: 'After all, you *see* it.' And it is this inner process that one means by the word 'remembering'. – The impression that we wanted to deny something arises from our setting our faces against the picture of the 'inner process'. What we deny is that the picture of the inner process gives us the correct idea of the use of the word 'to remember'. We say that this picture with its ramifications stands in the way of our seeing the use of the word as it is.[39]

We *can* make statements about pain, hope, remembering, in a sense. But they will only be either statements about ways in which we use the words 'pain', 'hope', 'remember'; or statements like 'there is a difference between pain behaviour with and without pain'. (' "But it seems as if you were neglecting something". But what more can I do than *distinguish* the case of saying "I have toothache" when I really have toothache, and the case of saying the words without having toothache.'[40])

Can't we, then, describe the inner life without setting up inner objects? Yes; we can say, for instance, 'I hope I'll win.' But in the 'label corresponding to an essence/object' sense, we can't describe it. 'Perhaps the word "describe" tricks us here. I say "I describe my state of mind" and "I describe my room". You need to call to mind the difference between the language-games.'[41] Describing one's state of mind is not listing publicly observable objects, so there are entirely different methods in each case for checking the truth of statements, learning how to describe, etc.

So, on the one hand there are inner experiences, and on the other statements about them. The statements, however, are not *about* the experiences in the way we feel we would like them to be. In the 'object-listing' sense, inner experiences are indescribable. There is a gap between words and 'inner experiences' which object-listing does not bridge. But the gap is created only by the wish to use object-listing language about inner experiences.

It will now, perhaps, begin to be clear how this fits in with the Mādhyamikas' Two Truths. Absolute truth and conventional truth are both the truth about the world. Neither are *false*. 'Because we accord with popular speech, there is no error. The Buddhas' Dharma-teaching always relies on the popular truth and on the absolute truth. Both these are true and not false speech.'[42] The conventional truth about inner experiences is expressed by the ordinary use of the relevant words. All that can validly be said, even when avoiding the object/essence point of view, is only conventional truth. The absolute truth about inner experiences is inexpressible, but not because it is the truth about a 'very special' kind of object – an experience not had by ordinary people. The two kinds of truth are both the truth about the same facts. To have understanding according to absolute truth is, however, superior, because it avoids all possibility of distortion by grammar, linguistic distinctions and common-sense assumptions.

Some Wider Comparisons

Suppose we think about seeing according to absolute truth as being direct and indescribable in the same way that 'private sensations' are indescribable for Wittgenstein. The chief disadvantage is that the comparison seems so impudent. Streng, who mentions certain similarities between Wittgenstein and Nāgārjuna, stresses the differences in their respective purposes. Wittgenstein's concern is 'for a small group of people interested in such problems – who call themselves philosophers – while for Nāgārjuna it is a religious concern which affects (and effects) the salvation of all existing beings.'[43] One advantage is that it helps us to understand the Mādhyamika, (which, for the purposes of the following section, I take to include the Prajñāpāramitā), without, if we are careful, distorting what they say. Let us see how the comparison works and, at the same time, briefly trace the connections between a few further comparisons, most of which will be dealt with more fully later on.

(a) *Wittgenstein*: Our experiences like hoping, remembering etc. are properly expressed in language as normally used, so long as we do not make them private sensations, and do not imagine that the word 'hope', for instance, must refer to something.

> Our wavering between logical and physical impossibility makes us make such statements as this: 'If what I feel is always *my* pain only, what can the supposition mean that someone else has pain?' The thing to do in such cases is always to look how the words in question *are actually used in our language*. We are in all such cases thinking of a use different from that which our ordinary language makes of the words.[44]

Mādhyamika: The absolute truth about what we conventionally call our 'inner life' is adequately expressed in language as long as we do not imagine dharmas to be distinct entities. 'Since there are no intrinsically different objects of knowledge, the distinction between "mundane truth" and "ultimate truth" does not pertain to different objects of knowledge e.g. the world and ultimate reality. It refers, rather, to the *manner* by which "things" are perceived.'[45] Even the phrase 'perfection of wisdom' does not refer to anything: '*Subhuti*: To call it "perfection of wisdom", O Lord, that is merely giving it a name. And what that name corresponds to, that cannot be got at. One speaks of a "name" with reference to a merely nominal entity. Even this perfection of wisdom cannot be found or got at.'[46] Yet this is *not* to say that we cannot satisfactorily talk of the perfection of wisdom. The passage continues: 'In so far as it is a word, in so far is it perfect wisdom; in so far as it is perfect wisdom, in so far is it a word. No duality of dharmas between these two can either be found or got at.'

(b) *Wittgenstein*: But there is a gap between words and experience which object-listing does not bridge, even though we'd like it to.

> Some things can be said about the particular experience and besides this there seems to be something, the most essential part of it, which cannot be described.... As it were: There is something further about it, only you *can't say* it; you can only make the general statement. It is this idea which plays hell with us.[47]

Mādhyamika: There is a gap between conventional and absolute truth. We cannot use words to express absolute truth, yet absolute truth can be 'conveyed' to another only by the use of words.[48]

(c) *Wittgenstein*: The 'gap' is illusory. It seemed to be there because we had a view of how words must refer to objects. 'What gives the impression that we want to deny anything? . . . Why should I deny that there is a mental process? . . . If I do speak of a fiction, then it is of a *grammatical* fiction.'[49] 'But don't you feel grief *now*? (But aren't you playing chess *now*?) The answer may be affirmative, but that does not make the concept of grief any more like the concept of a sensation.'[50]

Since there is really no gap between words and experience, it is important not to think of the indescribability of sensations, which I mentioned above, on the model of 'the mystical' in the Tractatus. Wittgenstein says there, for instance: 'There are, indeed, things that cannot be put into words. They *make themselves manifest*. They are what is mystical.'[51] But in the *Philosophical Investigations*, as van Peursen points out,

> What he had earlier called the mystical, the inexpressible, now permeates speech. So much so that speech becomes extremely elastic,

> interwoven with action and attitudes to life, and yet able to give expression to the mysterious questions of the soul, the 'I', attitudes, sympathy and hope – though not in the form of a description or theory.[52]

We cannot *describe* hope in the object-listing sense, but hope is certainly expressible.

Mādhyamika: The 'gap' (between absolute and conventional truth) is illusory. There *is no* gap according to absolute truth. The distinction was itself a result of the idea that words must refer to objects. The terms 'absolute truth' and 'conventional truth' do not refer to separate objects. 'The term "absolute truth" is part of the descriptive order, not part of the factual order.'[53] To see things according to absolute truth is to see 'things' as empty. If this is considered as something to be attained; if, that is, we consider that there is something which words don't properly express, then that is only because we had a view of how words must refer to objects. 'There is attainment, there is reunion, but not in the ultimate sense. But it is by means of worldly conventional expressions that one conceives of attainment and reunion, of streamwinners etc. to Buddha – but not in the ultimate sense.'[54]

This makes possible the following Mahāyāna equation of great renown:

> There is nothing whatever which differentiates the existence-in-flux (saṁsāra) from Nirvāṇa; And there is nothing whatever which differentiates Nirvāṇa from existence-in-flux. The extreme limit (koṭi) of Nirvāṇa is also the extreme limit of existence-in-flux; There is not the slightest bit of difference between these two.[55]

Streng comments: 'While it may be useful as a practical measure to distinguish between Saṁsāra and Nirvāṇa, it would be detrimental if one forgot that even these "things" do not exist apart from our giving them names.'[56]

(d) *Wittgenstein*: There is no way of 'rising above' language, no way of stepping outside *all* sets of assumptions about how things are, *all* forms of life, *all* language-games.[57] When we try to get at the 'neutral facts' expressible in different language-games, we keep coming up against a language-game and the set of assumptions to which it corresponds, and we can get no further.

Mādhyamika: The world as conceived according to conventional truth has structure imposed on it by language, and not vice versa. 'What human beings perceive as distinct entities or segments of existence is a result of mental fabrication. These entities, Nāgārjuna claims, do not exist in themselves; they exist because they are "named" –

distinguished from something else.'[58] But of course the perception of 'distinct entities or segments of existence' is a description of normality, not abnormality. In Wittgenstein's terms, *how* the world is divided up is part of what *constitutes* a 'form of life'.

(e) *Wittgenstein*: Yet philosophy stands above (or below) language-games. It can't be a language-game itself, nor within one. '"The word 'philosophy' must mean something which stands above or below, not beside the natural sciences" (Tractatus 4.111). In the *Investigations* we may replace "natural sciences" by "language-games".'[59]

Mādhyamika: 'These stanzas state that emptiness is not a term in the primary system referring to the world, but a term in the descriptive system (meta-system) referring to the primary system.'[60] To talk of emptiness is to stand above how we talk about the world. It includes talk about that talk. (It is to say, for instance, that how we talk about the world cannot be separated from our assumptions about entities in the world.)

(f) *Wittgenstein*: No theory is put forward. Since (as in (e)), 'Philosophy may in no way interfere with the actual use of language; it can in the end only describe it... It leaves everything as it is',[61] we can also say that 'In philosophy we do not draw conclusions. "But it must be like this!" is not a philosophical proposition. Philosophy only states what everyone admits.'[62] Philosophy does not involve advancing theses[63] or theories.[64]

Mādhyamika: 'Emptiness is proclaimed by the victorious one as the refutation of all viewpoints; But those who hold "emptiness" as a viewpoint – the true perceivers have called those "incurable" (asādhya).'[65]

'It is as if one were to ask, when told that there was nothing to give, to be given that nothing.'[66]

'If I would make any proposition whatever, then by that I would have a logical error; But I do not make a proposition; therefore I am not in error.'[67]

'Śāriputra, I therefore say that I do not see that dharma which could become clear to me as a dharma, or that by which it could become clear, or through which it could become clear, or wherein anything could become clear to me concerning anything.'[68]

In fact, the special quality of the Mādhyamika is generally taken to be that they criticise all possible philosophical views and theories without setting up anything in their place. Even the rejection of all views is not to be held on to as the 'correct' thing to do.

(g) *Wittgenstein*: Lack of theories is closely associated with the idea that since philosophy 'leaves everything as it is', one's need is to gain fresh insight into what is obvious. 'Philosophy simply puts everything before us, and neither explains nor deduces anything. – Since everything lies open to view, there is nothing to explain.'[69]

'The aspects of things that are most important for us are hidden because of their simplicity and familiarity. (One is unable to notice something – because it is always before one's eyes.)'[70]

Mādhyamika: In the same way, theory is unnecessary if the facts are faced. That is why emptiness, in its role as 'lack of views', is identified with Tathatā (suchness, that everything is as it is). 'Suchness alone lies outside the range of perverted knowledge.'[71]

(h) *Wittgenstein*: Getting rid of theories is like a medical cure. 'The philosophers treatment of a question is like the treatment of an illness.'[72] 'There is not *a* philosophical method, though there are indeed methods, like different therapies.'[73]

Mādhyamika: 'Of all theories, Kāśyapa, Śūnyatā is the antidote. Him I call the incurable who mistakes Śūnyatā itself as a theory (dṛṣṭi). It is as if a drug, administered to cure a patient, were to remove all his disorders, but were itself to foul the stomach by remaining therein.'[74]

Understanding what Pain is

The status of pain and how we ought to regard our understanding of a word like 'pain' are worth considering here, because pain is an important topic, for different reasons, for both Wittgenstein and the Mahāyāna.

When he needs an example of a private sensation, Wittgenstein uses pain more than he uses anything else. Pain is important for him because it has the best prima facie claim to being a private object which can be picked out and given a name to correspond to it; the best claim amongst putative private sensations, that is, to needing only a simple ostensive definition. Pains seem to be more like physical objects than are, for instance, hope, understanding or grief, because pains often have clear boundaries, both in time and space. One can, it seems, easily focus one's attention on a pain in a way which is difficult to do for, say, an 'act of understanding' or a 'sensation of hope'. And, of course, there is nothing *trivial* about pain as a philosophical example.

The Mahāyāna attack on pain as an ostensively definable private sensation is of particular importance for an entirely different reason. Pain (duḥkha) – the opposite of pleasure (sukha), dealt with above[75] – was the basis of the four holy truths. These form the backbone of Hīnayāna doctrine, although one hears rather less about them in the Mahāyāna, for reasons which will become apparent. The truths, briefly, are the truth that all conditioned dharmas have pain (duḥkha) as their 'mark' (lakṣana), the truth about the origination of pain, about the destruction of it and about the path to its destruction. The Abhidarmists saw evaluation as being expressed by the holy truths in a quite simple and literal way. One must progress from association with conditioned objects to the unconditioned object, Nirvāṇa. Nirvāṇa, unlike the conditioned world, has pleasure (sukha) as its mark. The term 'pleasure', as we have seen, does not, according to the Abhidharmists, refer to bodily sensations, but 'pain', although as an opposite of 'pleasure' it expresses 'disliked experience', also serves to express bodily pains. As 'disliked experience' it falls, with 'liked experience' (sukha), under the heading of the dharma 'feelings' (vedanā).

We can start looking at the Mahāyāna criticism of the foregoing by considering the famous statements in the *Heart Sutra* that feelings (along with the other four skandhas) do not differ from emptiness, and that where there is emptiness, or from the 'point of view' of emptiness, feelings cannot be regarded as real. This seems to throw doubt on the distinction between pain and pleasure and on whether it can be useful in helping to distinguish the conditioned world from Nirvāṇa. But it is not only liking/disliking which is denied objective status; so too is pain in its own right. If a pain is regarded as a real particular pertaining only to one person, there is a problem about how it is causally related to the person,[76] and in any case pain has no 'own-being'.[77] Denied reality as a particular by Nāgārjuna, pain is also denied reality as a 'mark' or quality of other experiences. The perfection of wisdom is said to pass beyond the consideration of what is marked with pain or pleasure.[78]

What, then, one might wonder, will have happened to the four noble truths? They cannot be said to be real either, says Nāgārjuna.[79] All that they stood for is absorbed into the 'truth of emptiness'.

'He who perceives dependent co-origination (*pratītya-samutpāda*) [which is also equated with emptiness[80]] also understands pain, origination and destruction, as well as the path.'[81]

Now, it is important to notice that to see things, including pain, as empty does not involve denying the occurrence of pleasure and pain. When one sees things as empty, one 'also understands pain.' To 'understand pain', for the Abhidharmists, was to be able to get conditioned dharmas properly into view as having a certain 'mark' or quality. For the Mādhyamikas, understanding what pain really is is still possible, still important, and still only fully possible from the standpoint of enlightenment. All this is so despite the fact that 'pain' designates nothing, and is not a 'quality of certain experiences'. To understand pain is no longer a matter of correctly apprehending certain dharmas; pain is understood *by* being seen as empty. Of course, the facts about liking and disliking, and about pleasure and pain, are not altered. But we no longer have to pretend, or need to imagine, that being able to understand what pleasure is involves comparing, say, a particular pleasure-sensation (pīti) with a dharma representing the 'essential pleasure sensation'. Nor that understanding what pain is involves having in mind a certain universal quality of painfulness or a kind of archetypal pain which can be seen to fit in a given case. Enlightenment is not now equated with a passage from object to object, but with a new way of understanding, among other things, pain and how we understand what it is.

When we come to consider Wittgenstein's attitude towards pain, we must remember that pain was for him a standard example of a private sensation, so that he has a greater number of different things to say about pain than one might expect. One of the most important points for our purposes, however, is the now familiar one that we cannot stick the word 'pain' directly on to a pain, for then a problem arises as to whether our sticking is accurate. We cannot have come to understand what 'pain' means by looking inside and discovering what bears the name,[82] and the same is true of what we might call the opposite of pain:

> 'But I do have a real *feeling* of joy! (Freude)' Yes, when you are glad you really are glad. And of course joy is not joyful behaviour, nor yet a feeling round the corners of the mouth and the eyes.
>
> 'But "joy" surely designates an inward thing.' No. 'Joy' designates nothing at all. Neither any inward nor any outward thing.[83]

As with Nāgārjuna, there is, of course, no suggestion that 'joy' or 'pain' do not mean anything. Quite the opposite: for us to be able properly to understand what they mean, we need to be freed from the twin ideas, that words can be granted meaning by simple ostensive definitions, and that understanding must be analysed in terms of confrontation with an object. Pain is what 'pain' means. Pain is empty because 'pain' designates nothing; (neither any inward nor outward thing). This changed view of what it is to understand a concept like pain can be expressed in general terms in various ways. One way of putting it is to say that a single kind of understanding is replaced by a multiplicity of kinds. Understanding, for Russell, occurs at the point of contact between a mind and an object in the external world.[84] It is a mental occurrence made possible by acquaintance with a particular or universal. For the Abhidharmists too, understanding stems from a clear confrontation with dharmas. Prajñā, often translated as 'understanding' as well as 'wisdom', is a mental dharma involving the 'getting into view' of (or 'getting acquainted with') all other dharmas. Set beside this, understanding for the Mādhyamikas and Wittgenstein seems to take various forms, because no single pattern is imposed on the various ways of understanding. Prajñāpāramitā, or seeing things as empty, replaces prajñā, or getting objects into view. Prapñāpāramitā is not a mental occurrence,[85] as the Abhidharmist prajñā was; it 'rises completely above all mental attitudes to dharmas,'[86] and Wittgenstein tells us to 'try not to think of understanding as a "mental process" at all.'[87] Further, seeing things as empty is, partly, to appreciate how words can come to have meaning in their different ways. In conventional truth – truth as expressed in language – meaning is founded on the way words are used, as we have seen. And there are lots of ways of using words – there are lots of language-games.

Another way of expressing the change is to say the opposite – that a multiplicity of kinds of understanding is replaced by one. Precisely *because* Russell and the Abhidharmists had wanted to put all examples of understanding on one level, they were obliged to create a number of separate departments for the odd cases which did not fit the confrontation pattern nicely. We saw how this happened to evaluation; special categories had to be opened by the atomists to include 'evaluational qualities'. Relations too became objects for understanding only at the cost of requiring the invention of a rather dubious neither-physical-nor-mental kind of existence. So there are different ways of understanding, in that the mind comes into contact with different kinds of object; and the differences had to be clearly maintained so that the plan of mind-confronting-object would not fall into absurdities. This diversity is replaced by a unity made possible by the toleration of language as actually used. All words are on one level, because they are all allowed to stand on their own feet. Different categories are not necessary since each word has, more or less, its own category. This helps to explain the fact that what is said in the Mahāyāna about emptiness is sufficient to do the job previously done by a great mass of piecemeal Hīnayāna teachings.

'Yes, it does the job,' you might want to say, 'but it no longer seems possible to understand a word clearly. Toleration of how words are actually used is all very well, but the meaning of a word – like pain for instance – seems fuzzy at the edges now. There don't seem to be any clear boundaries around pains to show what they are.'

But pains are not the objects with smooth perimeters the atomists had taken them to be. Discussing 'game', Wittgenstein points out that unless the concept is given rigid limits for a special purpose, there *are no* clear boundaries.

> For how is the concept of a game bounded? What still counts as a game and what no longer does? Can you give the boundary? No. . . . We do not know the boundaries because none have been drawn. . . . One might say that the concept 'game' is a concept with blurred edges. – 'But is a blurred concept a concept at all?' – Is an indistinct photograph a picture of a person at all? Is it even always an advantage to replace an indistinct picture by a sharp one? Isn't the indistinct one often exactly what we need?[88]

If, despite everything, we insist on trying to understand pain on the model of grasping an object, we will find ourselves faced with an object which is impossible to handle because it has no boundaries. This is equally true for the Mahāyāna. According to the *Perfection of Wisdom in 8000 Lines:*

> Perfect Wisdom is an infinite perfection because one cannot get at the beginning, middle or end of any objective fact (since as a dharma it has no own-being). Moreover, perfect wisdom is an infinite perfection because all objective facts are endless and boundless. . . . For one cannot apprehend the beginning, middle or end of form, *feelings* etc.[89] (My italics)

This 'boundlessness' of objective facts is not, it is stressed, a matter of there being a lot of them:

> *Sakra*: How is it, Holy Subhuti, that perfect wisdom is an infinite perfection by reason of the infinitude of beings?
> *Subhuti*: It is not so because of their exceedingly great number and abundance.
> *Sakra*: How then, Holy Subhuti, *is* perfect wisdom an infinite perfection by reason of the infinitude of beings?
> *Subhuti*: What factual entity does the word 'being' denote?
> *Sakra*: The word 'being' denotes no dharma or non-dharma. It is a term that has been added on (to what is really there) as something adventitious, groundless, as nothing in itself, unfounded in objective fact.
> *Subhuti*: Has thereby (i.e. by uttering the word 'being') any being been shown up (as an ultimate fact)?
> *Sakra*: No indeed, Holy Subhuti!
> *Subhuti*: When no being at all has been shown up, how can there be an infinitude of them?[90]

The thing to notice here is the reason which is given why the infinitude of beings is not an infinitude of objects. It is because the infinitude of beings is based on the fact that 'being' does not have meaning by denoting objects, which is not of course the same thing as saying that 'being' is a meaningless word. Nor for that matter is 'feelings' (vedanā) meaningless: they too are infinite in the same way. *Because* 'feelings' does not denote identifiable objects, feelings are infinite or boundless in a sense which has nothing to do with measuring or counting. The 'beginning, middle and end' of feelings which cannot be got at are not limits in space or time. Talking of limitlessness is a way of showing that one cannot encapsulate what 'feelings' means and that one cannot make feelings into an object. There is an infinitude of feelings for the Mahāyāna just as there is an 'infinitude of games' in the example from Wittgenstein. It is not that one could count for ever: it is that there are no traceable boundaries to the concept.

Why not Kant?

It may seem to some that interpreting the Mādhyamika in a Wittgensteinian way is an unimaginative and pointless task, because T. R. V. Murti has already[91] interpreted the Mādhyamika in a Kantian way, and Wittgenstein and Kant are in certain respects similar. It is true that there are many similarities between Wittgenstein and Kant. Wittgenstein's work can be seen as the 'second wave of critical philosophy,'[92] doing a job with language similar to the job Kant did with thoughts – finding the limits of what can be said (or thought) by an examination of language (or thought) itself. Both Kant and Wittgenstein make necessity and universality dependent on people's patterns of thought (or language). Both reject speculative metaphysics as the taking of thought (or language) on an illicit holiday beyond the limits of what can validly be thought (or said). But I do not think that the parallels between Wittgenstein and the Mādhyamika are simply a restating of Murti's ideas in more modern dress.

The problem with using Kantian ideas to interpret the Mādhyamika is that they give it a distastefully Absolutist flavour. For Murti, the term 'emptiness' refers to something – to an indescribable reality behind what we experience, to the Kantian Noumenon in fact. The mistake of not realising that the phrase 'emptiness of emptiness' tells us that 'emptiness' itself does not have meaning by referring to anything is the mistake common to two Western distortions of the idea of emptiness which have been noticed by Streng. They are: '1) emptiness seen as "nothing-ness", or 2) an absolute essence beyond every particular manifestation . . . The [second] alternative is represented by T. R. V. Murti and S. Schayer, who see the Mādhyamika dialectic as only preparatory for the intuition of the reality behind the illusory phenomena.'[93]

Murti says, for instance: 'The denial of the competence of Reason to have access to the real creates the duality of what appears in relation to the categories or *a priori* forms of thought (saṁvṛta – erscheinung), and what is in itself, the unconditioned (tattva, śūnya – Noumenon).'[94]

If, however, we think of the statement 'X is empty' as meaning something like '"X" doesn't refer', we can think of emptiness as 'the not being a referent and the having of no objective status', (despite the unpleasant crudities of this formulation). 'Emptiness of emptiness' *should*, then, remind us that we should not hypostatise emptiness. Murti, however, is led to interpret the phrase as 'The Unreality of (the knowledge of) Unreality,'[95] meaning by this only the rejection of all theories, including the 'theory of emptiness'. I do not say that this is unreasonable, but that it is only partial.

Once emptiness is made into a hidden reality, the essential idea of it has been lost. One might almost as well return to the Hīnayāna's realistic Nirvāṇa. Not quite, I admit, because the Hīnayānist Nirvāṇa is not a reality 'behind phenomena'. A great deal has been lost, however, if the Buddhist goal remains an object separate from the phenomena of ordinary experience, which is what it is both for the Abhidharmists and for Murti. And I do not see how this is to be avoided if one gives emptiness a primarily psychological (Kantian) interpretation rather than a linguistic (Wittgensteinian) one. Of course, the distinction between seeing everything as it is usually seen and seeing everything as empty is psychological rather than linguistic, but that is not what I mean. What I mean by a psychological interpretation of emptiness is what one finds if one looks, disregarding all the warnings, for an identifiable something corresponding to the term 'emptiness'. It clearly cannot be an item of ordinary experience and there is not even anything by which one might identify it. It also has to be something which somehow partakes of or is linked with *all* experiences, since everything is empty. All that seems to be left is an unexperienceable residue which remains when all that we actually experience is removed, a residue more real than the experiences in which it is cloudily dissolved. It is no longer a psychological entity exactly, because it 'underlies' normal experience without being part of it, yet is claimed to represent 'the unconditioned ground of phenomena'[96] – the Kantian Noumenon.

The freedom which is attainable by seeing everything as empty is not, as Murti imagines, the achievement of probing behind illusory phenomena to their real source or ground, but something quite different. Freedom, for the Mādhyamika, is not insight into any such 'grand facts', 'ultimate essence' or 'Absolute'. 'There is . . . a universally valid means for avoiding all claims to ultimacy, and this is the awareness of their emptiness.'[97] Seeing things as empty is offered as a way of freeing oneself *from* 'grand facts' and the like. It does not offer impressive answers to questions about what is the 'ground of phenomena' because it side-steps all such problems. 'This kind of soteriological "answer" is made possible by avoiding the assumption of a one-to-one correlation between a verbal expression and a non-lingual referent. The denial of an absolute reality operates to disintegrate a hierarchy of values based on an absolute "ground".'[98]

A Kantian approach to emptiness leads to just such an 'absolute ground'. A Wittgensteinian approach shows that the freedom which emptiness gives is freedom from assumptions about objects – assumptions based on a certain view of language. To know that X is empty is to know something about the way we can use and misuse language about X. But of course freedom is not simply a linguistic fact. The fact that I know that X is empty is a fact of psychology rather than of language. The human importance of understanding emptiness lies in that psychological fact and in its psychological implications, even though the fact that everything is empty is a linguistic rather than a psychological fact.

'Neither exists nor doesn't'

A Wittgensteinian interpretation of emptiness, then, avoids the false problem about what *kind* of an entity emptiness is. But it also avoids the need to say whether or not emptiness is an entity at all. It would be just as much of a mistake to say that emptiness *doesn't* exist as to say that it *does*. To use the word 'emptiness' is not to talk about the world in any way. It is to talk about how we talk about the world. To shift it from a lower to a higher order – from talk about the world to talking about talk about the world – is not to deny its importance, because 'emptiness' has a central position in the language-game where it belongs. Robinson says:

> These stanzas state that emptiness is not a term in the primary system referring to the world, but a term in the descriptive system (meta-system) referring to the primary system. Thus it has no status as an entity, nor as the property of an existent or an inexistent. If anyone considers it so, he turns the key term in the descriptive system into the root of all delusions.[99]

I shall retain Robinson's terminology in that I shall call the set of terms referring to the world the 'primary system' and the set of terms referring to the primary system the 'meta-system'. What Robinson is saying is that if something can meaningfully be said to exist or not to exist, the term for it must be in the primary system. If it turns out that a term must be placed in the meta-system, it would be nonsense to couple it with either existence or non-existence. Emptiness, then, neither exists nor doesn't. But emptiness isn't the only thing of which this can be said. We have already seen that the critics of the Abhidharmists tell us that *dharmas* neither exist nor don't. 'To what dharma could I point and say that "it is" or "it is not"? But a dharma which is absolutely isolated, to that one cannot attribute that "it is" or that "it is not".'[100] Yet surely the term 'dharma' belongs to the primary system? Something seems to be wrong here.

For the Abhidharmists, 'dharma' certainly did belong to the primary system. Dharmas were real objects, and the term 'dharma' corresponded to something real in the world, or, better, to everything real in the world. One could say it was the 'key term' in the primary system of the Abhidharmists. What, then, do their critics mean when they say that dharmas neither exist nor don't? Are they really suggesting that the term 'dharma' be promoted out of a useful job – be shifted from the primary system to the meta-system? It is hard to know what else one can say. The existence of dharmas is denied, yet the term 'dharma' is not suggested to be a self-contradiction like 'unmarried spouse', nor a term for something which simply happens not to exist, like 'unicorn'. When dharmas are denied, we are still left with a name which seems to have a use: it is just that it does not refer to anything. We can talk about dharmas, but we go wrong if we imagine that they exist, don't exist, have marks or in fact any properties of objects in the world. They are only 'talk', 'illustrated turns of speech' etc.

But how *can* the term 'dharma' belong to the meta-system? 'Emptiness' seems a straightforward case, since it was never meant to be the name of an object: it has always been a mistake to imagine it to belong to the primary system. 'Dharma', however, was definitely meant by the Abhidharmists to name real objects. Surely to talk of dharmas is to talk about the world and surely the only valid criticism of the Abhidharmist position is that it is mistaken talk about the world? No. It is a valid criticism to point out that what was thought to be the name of a real entity, an entity which must exist since it is defined as the simple, irreducible element of which all apparent existents are really composed, in fact only expresses the way we have come to talk about things. 'Nāgārjuna is especially concerned to show that the dharmas were not individual real entities which combined to construct sensuous existence – since they themselves were the product of the defining and distinguishing activity of human minds.'[101] Instead of being the 'key entities' corresponding to the 'key term' of the Abhidharmists' primary system, dharmas are now a model humanly constructed and embedded in the Abhidharmist language-game, a model which allows us to represent the world in a certain way (if we want to). For the Abhidharmists, dharmas *must* exist: for their critics, it is not true that dharmas must exist, because, we might say, their apparent necessity is rooted only in a certain (avoidable) language-game. One *can* talk in Abhidharmist terms, but the mistake lies in imagining that there are entities referred to by the term 'dharmas', or that distinctions between them are anything more than conventional.

Wittgenstein also says that the basic particulars of the analysts can be said neither to exist nor not to exist, although the position he is criticising is not quite the same as that of the Abhidharmists. This is because Wittgenstein is explicitly criticising a view held by Russell, which is that (Russellian) particulars neither exist nor don't, since a name has meaning only if it denotes an existent. To say that what is referred to by a name exists is to say that something which by definition exists, exists. (And of course particulars could not be said *not* to exist.) This differs from the Abhidharmists in that they (the Abhidharmists) claimed that dharmas *did* exist. They never suggested, as Russell did, that the basic particulars neither existed nor didn't. But this difference does not significantly undermine the parallels here, partly because Russell in less rigorous mood often talks of the existence of particulars (and it does seem rather strained to say that the 'super-existence' of particulars is not existence); and partly because the point of Wittgenstein's criticism is to *reinterpret* 'neither exists nor doesn't', not simply to accept it. And Wittgenstein's reinterpretation seems to me to express the same criticism of Russell's position on particulars as the criticism the Mādhyamikas make of the Abhidharmists' position on dharmas.

Before quoting the relevant passage from Wittgenstein, I had better mention that on the previous page (P.I. 48) he invents a language-game in which the red squares in a figure rather like chessboard are each called 'R'. We can, he emphasises, regard the coloured squares as 'simples' and the whole figure as 'composite', but this is a decision we have made, not something which is forced on us. (The words 'simple' and 'composite' have no single, absolute meanings outside a given language-game.[102]) That is what is referred to by 'language-game (48)' in the following:

> What does it mean to say that we can attribute neither being nor non-being to elements? . . . One would . . . like to say: existence cannot be attributed to an element, for if it did not *exist*, one could not even name it and so one could say nothing at all of it. – But let us consider an analogous case. There is *one* thing of which we can say neither that it is one metre long, nor that it is not one metre long, and that is the standard metre in Paris. – But this is, of course, not to ascribe any extraordinary property to it, but only to mark its peculiar role in the language-game of measuring with a metre-rule. – Let us imagine samples of colour being preserved in Paris like the standard metre. We define: 'sepia' means the colour of the standard sepia which is there kept hermetically sealed. Then it will make no sense to say of this sample either that it is of this colour or that it is not.
>
> We can put it like this: This sample is an instrument of the language used in ascriptions of colour. In this language-game it is not something that is represented, but is a means of representation. – And just this goes for an element in language-game (48) when we name it by uttering the word 'R': this gives this object a role in our language-game; it is now a *means* of representation. And to say 'If it did not *exist*, it could have no name' is to say as much and as little

> as: if this thing did not exist, we could not use it in our language-game. – What looks as if it *had* to exist, is part of the language. It is a paradigm in our language-game; something with which comparison is made. And this may be an important observation; but it is none the less an observation concerning our language-game – our method of representation.[103]

Wittgenstein is not here arguing *against* the idea that elements neither exist nor don't. He says that it *is* the case that elements neither exist nor don't, but that this has nothing to do with Russellian 'super-existence'. Elements neither exist nor don't, not because they *have* to exist, but because they are 'part of the language'. Elements are not 'something that is represented' (by terms in the primary system), but are 'a means of representation'. The term 'element', in so far as it 'stands for' anything, stands not for an object in the world, but for a way of talking about or a 'means of representation' of objects in the world. The term, therefore, takes a referential step backwards: it is transferred from the primary system to the meta-system.

There is remaining an apparent difficulty. Dharmas and emptiness are in the same boat: they neither exist nor don't. Yet there is obviously a sense in which the Mādhyamikas reject dharmas and accept emptiness. How is it, then, that it is more or less derogatory to say that dharmas neither exist nor don't, yet more or less complimentary to say it of emptiness?

The answer is that dharmas (and Russellian particulars, for that matter) were meant by their inventors to be real objects, so that their corresponding terms belong to the primary system. To say that the term 'dharma' belongs to the meta-system is insulting in that it no longer allows talk about dharmas to serve its original purpose. Atomism is not now a radical theory about what really exists, but a linguistic eccentricity. The term 'emptiness', on the other hand, was never meant to belong to the primary system. To say that emptiness neither exists nor doesn't is to avoid making the mistake of hypostatising it. It was always meant to belong to the meta-system.

It should not, by the way, surprise us that we find dharmas and emptiness on the same footing – neither existing nor not – because we have already seen that they are both empty. But here again, because of the wish of the Abhidharmists that 'dharma' should refer to something, to say that dharmas are empty has a certain flavour of insult (to dharmas at least), while the 'emptiness of emptiness' is a phrase of accuracy and glamour.

If we make as general as possible the point about the rejection of both the existence and non-existence of elements, we find ourselves back on familiar ground. For it now becomes a rejection of two apparently rivalling theories about language – one which Wittgenstein clearly rejects and one which he may be thought to put in its place. But in fact no theory is put forward. Pears says:

> [Wittgenstein] believed that the correct method was to fix the limit of language by oscillation between two points. In this case the outer point was the kind of objectivism which tries to offer an independent support for our linguistic practices, and the inner point is a description of the linguistic practices themselves, a description which would be completely flat if it were not given against the background of that kind of objectivism. His idea is that the outer point is an illusion, and that the inner point is the whole truth, which must, however, be apprehended through its contrast with the outer point. It is quite correct to apply the word 'anthropocentrism' to the inner point, provided that there is no implication that it is an alternative to objectivism.[104]

This suspension of theories, or oscillation between them, as Pears puts it, has already been mentioned. One can escape here from a seemingly inevitable choice between objectivism and subjectivism; between the theory that objects are independently real and that they are a function of people's feelings, opinions, etc. about them. Such escapes, as we have also seen, are like a cure. This is also the case in the Mādhyamika: realising that one can suspend rival theories about the real existence or the non-existence of objects is the medicine.

'When neither existence nor non-existence is presented again to the mind, then, through lack of any other possibility, that which is without support becomes tranquil.'[105]

4 Yogācāra Contributions

Mādhyamika and Yogācāra

The Mādhyamika and the Yogācāra are the two main Mahāyāna schools. The difference of approach is nicely summed up by Conze:

> Mādhyamikas and Yogācārins supplement one another. . . . To the Mādhyamikas 'wisdom' is everything and they have very little to say about *dhyāna*, whereas the Yogācārins give more weight to the experiences of 'trance'. The first annihilate the world by a ruthless analysis which develops from the Abhidharma tradition. The second effect an equally ruthless withdrawal from everything by the traditional method of trance.[1]

One might expect little interest to be shown by the Yogācāra in the problem of entanglement by language, but this is not the case. In the Lankāvatāra Sutra, for instance, there is considerable stress laid on our attachment to linguistic discrimination and its binding power, holding us back from salvation. This Sutra is a work probably predating the formation of the Yogācāra as a separate school, but is generally regarded as expressing a Yogācāra point of view. There is certainly no conflict between the attitude to words found in the Sutra and the attitude of the Mādhyamikas which we have been considering. It is interesting, however, to look at some of the Lankāvatāra Sutra's statements about language, because the same Mahāyāna position is expressed, but with little or no mention of emptiness, which figures so largely in the Mādhyamika.

To start with, words do not necessarily derive meaning by referring: 'Said the Blessed One: Even when there are no (corresponding) objects there are words, Mahāmati; for instance, the hare's horns, the tortoise's hair, a barren woman's child etc. – they are not at all visible in the world but the words are; Mahāmati, they are neither entities nor nonentities but expressed in words.'[2]

And words can without any loss be replaced by non-linguistic pieces of behaviour. (Cf. Wittgenstein's suggestion that 'words are connected with the primitive, the natural, expressions of the sensation and used in their place.'[3]) The Sutra continues:

> If, Mahāmati, you say that because of the reality of words the

objects are, this talk lacks in sense. Words are not known in all the Buddha-lands; words, Mahāmati, are an artificial creation. In some Buddha-lands ideas are indicated by looking steadily, in others by gestures, in still others by a frown, by the movement of the eyes, by laughing, by yawning, or by the clearing of the throat, or by recollection, or by trembling.

The unwise separate the world into objects according to the different names of things; this separation is called 'discrimination' (vikalpa):

Said Mahāmati: How is it that the ignorant are given up to discrimination and the wise are not?

Said the Blessed one: Mahāmati, the ignorant cling to names, ideas and signs; their minds move along (these channels). As thus they move along, they feed on multiplicity of objects, and fall into the notion of an ego-soul and what belongs to it, and cling to salutory appearances.[4]

Further, Mahāmati, by 'discrimination' is meant that by which names are declared, and there is thus the indicating of (various) appearances. Saying that this is such and no other, for instance, saying that this is an elephant, a horse, a wheel, a pedestrian, a woman, or a man, each idea thus discriminated is so determined.[5]

Further, Mahāmati, word-discrimination cannot express the highest reality, for external objects with their multitudinous individual marks are non-existent, and only appear before us as something revealed out of Mind itself. Therefore, Mahāmati, you must try to keep yourself away from the various forms of word-discrimination.[6]

There is an obvious objection to this. If word-discrimination is so pernicious, why was the Lankāvatāra Sutra (and all the rest) written at all? And, worse still, why did the Buddha give spiritual advice on how to achieve salvation, advice necessarily given in words? One answer to this objection is that the Buddha never spoke at all. Beginning with the Mahāsaṅghikas, this idea keeps cropping up in the Mahāyāna, and is certainly there in the Lankāvatāra.[7] The other answer to the objection is, while admitting that absolute reality cannot be *expressed* in words, to claim that words can help one towards salvation. The Mādhyamikas express this by saying that absolute truth cannot be taught without conventional truth.[8] The Lankāvatāra employs this answer too, in different language. Words are quite satisfactory as long as they are kept in their proper place. Their proper place is to be used as tools (for enlightenment), not as labels. It is all too easy to think of a firm distinction between Saṁsāra and Nirvāṇa, falsehood and truth, undesirable and desirable, and to cast words emphatically on the side of the villains. We have seen, however, that this is not the Mahāyāna attitude. All that is wrong with words is our attachment to using them as labels, to making absolute discriminations. In the next extract from the Lankāvatāra, the Buddha talks about the relation between *ruta* and *artha*. 'Ruta' means 'word', and 'artha', translated by Suzuki as 'meaning' in the extract, also means 'reality' or 'what is of value'.

> Further, Mahāmati, the Bodhisattva-Mahāsattva who is conversant with words and meaning observes that words are neither different nor non-different from meaning and that meaning stands in the same relation to words. If, Mahāmati, meaning is different from words, it will not be made manifest by means of words; but meaning is entered into by words as things (are revealed) by a lamp. It is, Mahāmati, like a man carrying a lamp to look after his property. (By means of this light) he can say: This is my property and so is kept in this place. Just so, Mahāmati, by means of the lamp of words and speech originating from discriminations, the Bodhisattva-Mahāsattvas can enter into the exalted state of self-realization which is also free from speech-discrimination.[9]

So words are like a lamp. They do not conceal reality, but reveal it. What is interesting in the above passage is that, since 'artha' covers both 'meaning' and 'reality', reality is 'what words mean'. And yet we must not think of meaning/reality as something separate from words. That would lead straight back to all the rigours and horrors of the idea that the meaning of words can always be discovered by finding what they refer to. 'If, Mahāmati, meaning is different from words, it will not be made manifest by means of words.' Wittgenstein says: 'This again is connected with the idea that the meaning of a word is an image, or a thing correlated to the word. (This roughly means, we are looking at words as though they were proper names, and we then confuse the bearer of a name with the meaning of the name.)'[10]

This is not to say, of course, that words and meanings are the same. Words in themselves are only combinations of sounds or letters. But by the *use* of words, meaning is shown. Words, like lamps, are revelatory when used; they are both tools. Tools are for doing things with. Too much respect for the tools as independent objects detracts from their usefulness. We are liable to project the distinctions between words on to the world as absolute distinctions between separate objects. This is 'discrimination':

'Those who, following words, discriminate and assert various notions, are bound for hell because of their assertions. . . . The reality of objects is seen being discriminated by the ignorant; if it were so as they are seen, all would be seeing the truth.'[11]

'Word-discrimination cannot express the highest reality, for external objects with their multitudinous marks are non-existent.'[12]

Universals

So far, it cannot be said that there is, in all of this, anything really different from the Mādhyamika position. (After all, 'the perfection of wisdom does not make any discriminations'[13] either.) But in the later Yogācāra, there appeared a school of logicians represented chiefly by Dignāga, Dharmakīrti and Dharmottara, who expressed some of the Yogācāra views on words in more purely logical terms. Most important for us is their attitude to *universals*. Although the Abhidharmists made universals into objects of acquaintance, there are signs, as we have seen, that even within the Hīnayāna fold, the Mahāsaṅghikas felt uneasy about it. The Abhidharmists' realism about universals was completely rejected by the Buddhist logicians. Stcherbatsky says of them: 'The static universality of things [is] replaced by similarity of action.'[14] 'There is in the things themselves [i.e. particulars] not a bit of common substance.'[15]

'The Universals [sāmānya-lakṣaṇa] . . . (although they can be named) are not (external) realities, they are not real objects. And this is just the reason why the absolute particulars do not *possess* them. Since the Universals do not exist . . . neither does their 'possession' by the particulars also really exist.'[16]

Wittgenstein also rejects realism about universals. There is

> the tendency to look for something in common to all the entities which we commonly subsume under a general term. – We are inclined to think that there must be something in common to all games, say, and that this common property is the justification for applying the general term 'game' to the various games; whereas games form a *family* the members of which have family likenesses. Some of them have the same nose, others the same eyebrows and others again the same way of walking; and these likenesses overlap.[17]

Now, if games have not got in common a real universal, a general quality or essence of 'gameness' constituting a minimum qualification for being a game, what they *have* got in common must be something rooted in human decision or classification. Different classifications (or 'discriminations', as the Lankāvatāra says) are possible, and in the final analysis it is people who do the classifying. Distinctions are not made in heaven for all time. This anthropocentric attitude to the distinctions between things was mentioned above[18] when I was comparing Wittgenstein with the Mādhyamikas. But what is important to notice now is that when we come to consider universals, it is anthropocentrism which is the only alternative to realism. What is *usually* taken to be the only alternative to realism is *nominalism*, the theory that games, for instance, have in common only the word 'game'. Nominalism certainly is one variety of anthropocentrism about universals – people create words and apply them to objects – but it is not the only one. The other variety, the third alternative, is, I shall argue, adopted by the Buddhist logicians. As adopted too by Wittgenstein, it is explained by Renford Bambrough:

> The nominalist says that games have nothing in common except that they are called games. The realist says that games must have something in common, and he means by this that they must have something in common other than that they are games. Wittgenstein says that games have nothing in common except that they are games.[19]

Once we have classified things in a certain way, let us say as being *blue*, then it is not enough to say that blue things have in common only a word. Pears says:

'The way in which our language divides up the range of colours is not the only possible way, but, when it is done in this way, that necessary truth is automatically written into the rules for our use of colour words.'[20]

In Wittgensteins words:

'Should you say we use the word "blue" both for light blue and dark blue because there is a similarity between them? If you were asked "Why do you call this 'blue' also?", you would say "Because this *is* blue, too." '[21]

> Now what should we answer to the question 'What do light blue and dark blue have in common?'? At first sight the answer seems obvious: 'They are both shades of blue.' But this is really a tautology. So let us ask 'What do these colours I am pointing to have in common?' (Suppose one is light blue, the other dark blue.) The answer to this really ought to be 'I don't know what game you are playing.'[22]

'To say that we use the word "blue" to mean "what all these shades of colour have in common" by itself says nothing more than that we use the word "blue" in all these cases.'[23]

It is obvious that this comes pretty close to nominalism, but Wittgenstein also implies that, although our classifications, of colour for instance, seem arbitrary in a way, they *are* objective. This objectivity can be approached in two ways. First, underlying any classification there is a pattern of similarities. There are similarities between all blue things, for example. But there is no 'one big similarity', one essence of blue, shared by them all. Secondly, if we are to talk of things at all, we must use words and the classifications they represent. There is nothing we can say about the world before any classification. We cannot escape from *all* language-games and 'forms of life', and whichever one we adopt involves implicit classifications. In this second sense, a classification is objective in that it is unavoidable within a given language-game. Once we have classified things as blue and yellow, we are obliged to say that this *is* blue and that that *is* yellow, not merely that they are given the names 'blue' and 'yellow'.

Stcherbatsky, having discussed realism about universals, and corresponding definitions in terms of the possession of 'essences', says of the Buddhist logicians:

> The Buddhists contended that such definitions are useless, since the 'essences' do not exist. For them the characteristic feature of all our conceptual knowledge and of language, of all nameable things and of all names, is that they are dialectical . . . all our definitions are concealed classifications, taken from some special point of view. . . . What the colour 'blue' is e.g., we cannot tell, but we may divide all colours into blue and non-blue. . . . The definition of blue will be that it is not non-blue and, *vice versa*, the definition of non-blue that it is not the blue.[24]

What blue things have in common, then, according to the Buddhist logicians, is that none of them are non-blue. Stcherbatsky refers to this theory (apoha-vāda) as Nominalism, but this title fits the logicians as well and as badly as it fits Wittgenstein. Blue things have in common more than just a word, because to use a word is to use the classification behind it. The logicians do not suggest that classifications and words are all invalid or all nonsense. In the usual Mahāyāna style, they draw a distinction between seeing reality as it really is (in its Suchness) and seeing it according to our classifications or 'discriminations' based on words. But 'the unutterable reality can nevertheless be designated, of course indirectly, by names, and it becomes incumbent upon the author of the drama to represent the behaviour of Names towards Reality, to establish the part of reality they indirectly can touch.'[25]

The 'part of reality they indirectly can touch' is reality as classified in some way. We can express this by saying that names correspond to universals, as long as 'universal' here does not imply any kind of realism. Given that assumption, it is even a useful way of putting it, because it is yet another way of steering away from a referential theory of meaning.

'Language is not a separate source of knowledge and names are not the adequate or direct expressions of reality. Names correspond to images or concepts, they express only Universals. As such they are in no way the direct reflex of Reality, since reality consists of particulars, not of universals.'[26]

For both the Buddhist logicians and Wittgenstein, then, a word like 'blue' sums up a human classification of experience which might have been done in another way. Since lots of things can be classified as blue, we can, if we like, say that 'blue' is a name for a universal, but Wittgenstein and the logicians are equally hostile to a realism about universals. The (not simply nominalistic) anthropocentrism, which is what we are left with, seems weak in a way and strong in another. It seems weak because all classifications are, in a sense, arbitrary. A totally arbitrary classification, of course, in which none of the items were linked by *any* similarity, would not be a classification at all. No, they seem arbitrary because a different classification is always possible. We saw this above in Pears' remarks about Wittgenstein on colour, and it is admitted also by the Buddhist logicians. Vācaspatimiśra says that a name 'is arbitrarily applied to an object.'[27] And when his opponent, the realist, is made to say that 'names are associated with things as a consequence of an arbitrary agreement',[28] he agrees that the use of names is founded on arbitrary agreement, but points out, in consistency with his school's views on names and universals, that the 'agreement' is not so much about names and things as about names and universals. '(Humanity) has concluded an agreement exclusively concerning Universals',[29] which are alone represented by names, as we have seen, and are themselves 'concealed classifications'. If this arbitrariness is a weakness, it is only one by contrast with realism, according to which we can look behind the distinction between words like 'blue' and 'yellow' to an objective distinction rooted in the facts, discovered rather than created by people.

And that is just where its strength lies. There is no need to 'look behind' a term for the objective universal it refers to, and so no puzzlement about why the colour-range, for instance, *must* be divided up in the way it is and not in another way. We can come to certainty about whether a thing is blue by looking at our use of the word 'blue' (and the classification underlying it), instead of, like the realists, looking for an identifiable essence of blueness common to all blue things.

What, then, about the difference between Wittgenstein's approach and that of the logicians? Wittgenstein says, to use Bambrough's shorthand style, that blue things have nothing in common except that they are all blue. The Buddhist logicians say that blue things have nothing in common except that none of them are non-blue. Why is this double negative used when a simple positive statement would apparently serve just as well?

According to Stcherbatsky, it is a way of making clear the total rejection of realism. Once any objective similarity between two items is admitted, there is the danger of freezing the similarity into an entity distinct from the items. He says:

'There is between [particulars] no similarity at all, but by neglecting all their difference and by a common contrast we can identify them.... If there were no objects with which they could be contrasted they would be quite dissimilar.'[30]

If *everything* were blue, and the same shade of blue, we would not have the word 'blue' nor any other word with the same meaning. There would, obviously, be no colour-words at all. The word 'blue', like all words, has a meaning and is useful only when it plays its part in a language-game. Wittgenstein, in the Brown Book, talks about what moment of time the word 'now' could possibly refer to:

> The function of the word 'now' is entirely different from that of a specification of time. – This can easily be seen if we look at the role this word really plays in our usage of language, but it is obscured when instead of looking at the *whole language-game*, we only look at the contexts, the phrases of language in which the word is used.[31]

One reaction to this is to say that 'now' is not perhaps a typical word so far as dependence on its place in a language-game is concerned. If we are to credit the realist with intelligence, we must pick examples in which there is a clearer case of a word which apparently refers to a single entity, a simple labelling process. Isn't it possible to ascribe a name to a thing without the name being part of a public language at all? Surely we can find a safe example in which one gives something a name quite privately. But then we are back with the difficulties of a private language. How can one be sure one always uses the word in the same way? How can there be rules for the use of the word? Wittgenstein sets out a *reductio ad absurdum* of the attempt to confer labels outside any language-game. He imagines a case where someone picks out a particular sensation and calls it 'S':

> What reason have we for calling 'S' the sign for a *sensation*? For 'sensation' is a word of our common language, not intelligible to me alone. So the use of this word stands in need of a justification which everybody understands. – And it would not help either to say that it need not be a *sensation*; that when he writes 'S', he has *something* –

and that is all that can be said. 'Has' and 'something' also belong to our common language. – So in the end when one is doing philosophy one gets to the point where one would like just to emit an inarticulate sound. – But such a sound is an expression only as it occurs in a particular language-game, which should now be described.[32]

The Buddhist logicians, I want to suggest, want to stress the fact that to use a word is not to express a single 'meaning' hanging in mid-air. To express what one means *is* to implicitly distinguish it from what other words mean. From a summary of Dignāga:

> Just for this reason the word does not accomplish two different jobs, viz. the repudiation of the discrepant meaning and the positive statement of one's own meaning. Since the essence of one's own meaning of a word consists in its being different from other meanings. As soon as it is expressed, we feel straight off that the contrary is rejected.... (The objection has been made) that if the word will have exhausted its function by repelling the contrary, we will be obliged to find another word in order to express its positive import. But this is a mistake, since the word *eo ipso* repels the contrary. Indeed a word by merely suggesting its own meaning, suggests also the repudiation of everything discrepant, because this suggested (negative) meaning is inseparable (from the positive one).[33]

I do not say, of course, that the point made here is identical to that made by Wittgenstein in the passage quoted from him. What I am arguing is that since both had rejected realism about universals – and this, surely, is not in dispute – they were led to a similar view about how words relate to each other. The realism which was rejected had involved the idea that a word like 'blue' corresponds to or refers to a single something which constitutes its essential meaning, muddied perhaps in actual applications of the word. Once this idea has gone, from where can words derive their meaning? Only from their position in a public language; from what use people make of them. To define 'blue', there is no single thing one can point out as that to which the word refers. Lots of different shades of colour are blue, and lots of things of the same shade of blue are blue. What the shades or the blue things have in common is *partly* that the word 'blue' can be used of them all – the nominalist's point. But only partly, because the printed sign – 'blue' – wouldn't have any meaning at all if there weren't words for other colours, and also places in language for other colour-words; that is, ways for us to use them. In a way, one might say that all words are interdefined, if we understand 'defined' in a rather loose sense. If we try to say what 'blue' really means, we come eventually to the word's relations to other words, and not to something independent of language, to which we must try to link our word.

Wittgenstein sees this interrelatedness as a co-operating system. 'Our' language-games are 'human', needed by us, and we ought to feel relaxed in them, not neurotically trying to pick out individual features, hoping they will live after being uprooted. Words are related in a language-game quite naturally and harmoniously. The Buddhist logicians take a more aggressive line. Words need each other like a boxer needs other boxers. A word derives its meaning by carving out a place for itself.

It does not seem to me that there is any important logical difference between the two approaches. In avoiding a referential norm of meaning, they are both in agreement with Nāgārjuna's 'insistence that the meaning of words i.e. "names" is derived from the relationship which one word has with other words, not from an intrinsic relationship with an existent objective referent.'[34]

5 Others and Myself

After the escape from the Russellian/Abhidharmist primacy of privacy, it is not surprising that *people* reappear on the scene. But the way in which they are welcomed back is remarkable. Apart from specific arguments about personal identity, people are now *assumed* to exist from the start; and the whole question of whether, for example, the term 'I' refers to something or nothing is thrown out altogether.

There are various facets of anthropocentrism and populism (for want of a better term) in Wittgenstein and the Mādhyamika. We have already seen that language as used by real people takes over the position held by the kind of uses of language allowed by the analysts. Not only quasi-scientific descriptions of what is 'non-superficially' the case are to be regarded as valid, but now all actual uses of words, descriptive or otherwise. A variety of linguistic élitism has been done away with. No longer can people be told that the correct analysis of 'book' leaves out some of what one normally means by 'book'; quite the other way. What one normally means by 'book' (that is, how the word 'book' is normally made use of) is what is inescapable. Philosophy cannot now claim to give any information. In particular, speculative metaphysics is sham. While stressing their different purposes, Streng points out that 'both Wittgenstein and Nāgārjuna maintain that metaphysical systems are mental constructs produced to a large extent from an extension of functional relationships of words.'[1] Wittgenstein says that 'the characteristic of a metaphysical question [is] that we express an unclarity about the grammar of words in the *form* of a scientific question.'[2]

That is just how the Abhidharmists had created their dharmas. The real facts of the situation can be got at by discovering what words refer to. If they do not seem to refer to anything, then one must focus one's philosophical microscope more carefully until the objects come into view.

'Systems of philosophy have merely universalised the scientific method and given free scope to the flight of imagination.... The Mādhyamika system is unique in this respect that it rejects the scientific or literary method of explanation and speculative construction as utterly unsuited to philosophy.'[3]

The Importance of People

The therapeutic, 'curing of theories',[4] value of the Wittgensteinian and

Mādhyamika critiques stands in opposition to what had gone before. The aim of both is not to give information, but to *free people* from a view of the world in which what had looked like information turns out to be nothing but grammar treated as science. The 'objective searcher for truth' image, or at least one version of it, does not fit here. Neither Wittgenstein nor Nāgārjuna would have been content simply to arrive at a statement about what they considered to be true. They had to publish! Illnesses are not cured by having the remedy kept safe in the bank.

It is perhaps all too easy to stress, as Streng does, the different groups for which the two men wrote. Although they may come to a comparable philosophical conclusion, says Streng,[5] Nāgārjuna is concerned with everyone's salvation, while Wittgenstein is interested only in other philosophers. It is true that religious and academic aims may be contrasted, but there is more to be said.

First, could it be claimed that it is only people calling themselves philosophers who assume the existence of private sensations, pains, hopes etc. which can be internally pointed to and named? And only philosophers who misleadingly transfer pictures and models from one language-game to another? Clearly not; Wittgenstein may best be understood in relation to the philosophical theories against which he reacted, but his criticism of them extends to criticism of the commonsense ideas of many or all non-philosophers. Pitcher remarks:

> One might get the impression that, according to Wittgenstein, it is only philosophers who have such pictures of things. This, however, is not his view. He claims that we all have them, that they are entirely natural, being the product of causes which operate on all men, not just on philosophers. The underlying causes of the trouble-making pictures are connected with language itself, according to Wittgenstein.[6]

Secondly, as in the case of Wittgenstein, to understand Nāgārjuna properly one has to understand his predecessors – in his case the Abhidharmists. And although Nāgārjuna dealt with matters affecting everyone, he did not write for everyone. His *Mādhyamikakārikās*, for instance, is universally admitted not to be an easy work; hardly a 'popular book'. The set of people for whom a book (by Wittgenstein, Nāgārjuna, or anybody else) is intended is quite distinct from the set of people who would be affected if they heeded its contents.

Third, there are indications that Wittgenstein himself saw his work as being of benefit not only to professional philosophers but to anyone, and also as benefitting people in a more important way than one is accustomed to expect from philosophers.[7] There is not nearly as much difference between the roles of Wittgenstein and Nāgārjuna as one might imagine. Both of them fit rather uncomfortably into their respective traditions just to the extent that they approach one another. Crudely, the Mādhyamikas represent a philosophical trend of the Buddhist religion; Wittgenstein represents a religious trend of 'British' philosophy. By saying 'a religious trend', I do not mean that Wittgenstein's philosophy can somehow be interpreted as a religion, but that there are certain aspects of his attitude to his philosophy which do remind one of a 'philosophical religion' like the Mādhyamika.

K. T. Fann, for instance, compares Wittgenstein with a Zen master. One has to be led to dissatisfaction and perplexity about a philosophical problem before one can be liberated. And this is not just to make the obvious remark that one must have a problem before it can be solved:

> 'Before you have studied Zen, mountains are mountains and rivers are rivers; while you are studying it, mountains are no longer mountains and rivers are no longer rivers; but once you have had Enlightenment, mountains are once again mountains and rivers are rivers.' Something is gained by this process i.e. enlightenment.[8]
>
> The state of 'enlightenment' in which the mind is free from philosophical questions is not unlike the state of 'complete clarity' which Wittgenstein was searching for.[9]

Wittgenstein certainly offers *liberation*: 'A picture held us captive'[10] – 'What is your aim in philosophy? – To shew the fly the way out of the fly-bottle.'[11]

The liberation is from a spell cast by obsession of certain pictures of how things must be, as suggested by grammar: 'Philosophy is a battle against the bewitchment of our intelligence by means of language.'[12] 'Philosophy, as we use the word, is a fight against the fascination which forms of expression exert on us.'[13]

But the only way to come to realise how bewitched we are is to bring the bewitchment to a head in philosophical puzzlement. 'You had confusions you never thought you could have had.'[14] In the Mādhyamika, one often reads that everything is illusion, but this does not mean empirical illusion – on the model of optical mistakes and the like. It is the bewitchment which leads eventually to philosophical impasse. Murti says,

> The Mādhyamika dialectic, being a criticism of philosophical standpoints, can get under way only when the different systems have already been formulated.... The world-illusion is presented to the Mādhyamika as the total and persistent conflict of Reason – the interminable opposition of philosophical viewpoints.[15]

The problems to which we have been led are, however, only pseudo-problems: 'Foolish, untaught, common people have settled down in them [the dharmas]. Although they do not exist, they have constructed all the dharmas.'[16] 'So too in the Investigations: the difficulties are unreal ones which we have created for ourselves, and when we see things aright, the problems vanish as if by magic.'[17] (And 'The real discovery is the one that makes me capable of stopping doing philosophy when I want to.'[18])

Wittgenstein, then, offered liberation of a kind which Western philosophers have not normally offered. And he felt, apparently, that his work ought to be appreciated as making a difference to people. His was not merely the usual academic philosophy which left one as it found one.

> Wittgenstein insisted that philosophical encounter with him produced moral change. In a moving part of his memoir of Wittgenstein, his student Norman Malcolm reports how bitterly Wittgenstein complained when this did not happen: 'What is the use of studying philosophy', Wittgenstein once asked, 'if all that it does for you is to enable you to talk with some plausibility about some abstruse questions of logic etc. and if it does not improve your thinking about the important questions of everyday life?'[19]

Elsewhere in the same memoir, Malcolm tells us that he had made a remark to Wittgenstein about the 'British national character' but: 'my remark made him extremely angry. He considered it to be a great stupidity and also an indication that I was not learning anything from the philosophical training that he was trying to give me.'[20]

Wittgenstein insisted that his lectures must be attended only by those serious-minded enough to come regularly – ('My lectures are not for tourists.'[21]) And when he was a teacher in an Austrian village, he told a villager that 'although he was not a Christian, he was an "evangelist". The villager was bewildered, for Wittgenstein emphasised that he did not mean he was a Protestant (or "Evangelical").[22] The villager was in good company, for many others have been bewildered by Wittgenstein's evangelistic traits. If his work is thought of, as it often has been, as part of the mainstream of English philosophy, these characteristics necessarily look like signs of mere arrogance, and are liable to be ignored by Wittgenstein's admirers. It is possible that they are partly accounted for by arrogance, but it seems likely that (in contrast with followers of the English tradition of empiricism derived from Locke, Berkeley and Hume), Wittgenstein wished to change people in a more genuine and radical way than would those philosophers whose aim is, primarily, the correct description of the world.

I do not intend to offer evidence that the aim of the Mādhyamika was to liberate people in some way, since that is so obviously assumed in all Buddhist schools: it is what Buddhism as a whole is all about. But in the case of, say, Nāgārjuna, there are almost no *other* clues to his being a 'religious' writer:

> Nāgārjuna's expression of 'emptiness' as the term articulating Ultimate Truth, is an extreme example of nondevotional Buddhism. If the assertion of an absolute (divine) Being is a requisite for 'religious' thinking, then Nāgārjuna's affirmation of 'emptiness' can be regarded merely as an interesting philosophical position of extreme scepticism. We, however, have interpreted this expression as religious on the ground that *it has a soteriological intention.*[23]

This common aim of effecting a practical change is associated with a close similarity in the methods found appropriate to it. The ways of getting people to understand what they need to understand can be most easily explained if we go back for a moment to the discussion[24] of what the analysts and their critics took 'understanding' to be. For the former, it will be remembered, understanding is the confrontation of the mind with whatever is to be understood. To get someone to understand something, therefore, is a matter of presenting him with the facts. What the philosopher should be doing, according to Russell, is making the attempt, however difficult in practice, to present the reader with indubitable knowledge, such as that of our sense-data.[25] The reader either sees the truth as presented to him and accepts it (not necessarily on trust, of course), or else he doesn't see it, in which case there is not much that can be done. The exposition of the truth according to Hīnayāna Buddhism is the task, centrally, of the Buddha. In the Sutras, he sets out his teachings, the truth of which has to be 'seen'. Arguments are put forward, certainly, but in the final analysis the Buddha's doctrine is a 'come-and-see-thing'[26] – it is a matter of 'take it or leave it'. This rather alarming spirit of tolerance is merely consistent with the idea of an act of understanding being rooted in a basic act of seeing. Either one sees or one does not.

For Wittgenstein, getting people to understand is much more than presenting them with the facts. He is prepared to use any means in accordance with what works best. There are no irreducible acts of understanding and therefore no 'ultimate explanations'. Rather, 'an explanation serves to remove or to avert a misunderstanding – one, that is, that would occur but for the explanation; not every one that I can imagine.'[27] An explanation need not be the 'presentation of facts' at all – it could be a gesture or pricking someone with a pin.[28] In different cases, different measures are called for, if liberation is to be achieved: 'Philosophy unties knots in our thinking; hence its result must be simple, but philosophising has to be as complicated as the knots it unties.'[29] And, as we know, there are different methods in philosophy, 'like different therapies.'[30] So isn't Wittgenstein's concern as a philosopher that of setting out his arguments and letting the reader make up his mind about them? Far from it: 'I am in a sense making propaganda for one style of thinking as opposed to another. I am honestly disgusted with the other.'[31]

In Buddhism, one of the important differences between Hīnayāna and Mahāyāna lies precisely in this problem of how to get people to understand, how to help them to be liberated. The Mahāyāna attitude is summed up in the concept of *skill in means* (upāya-kauśalya). This skill is an achievement of the Bodhisattva, the Mahāyāna liberator, who uses it to help others to attain Nirvāṇa. Any method which works may be used, although a Bodhisattva's wisdom is necessary to enable one to know which will work in practice: 'The skill in means of the Bodhisattvas should be known as having come forth from the perfection of wisdom.'[32] Those who employ skill in means often, like Wittgenstein, resort to 'unphilosophical' tricks to force people into a position from where it is harder to avoid understanding the point. Skill in means involves a very wide range of skills indeed, including the ability to conjure up phantom bodies; but the use of beneficial and opportunist trickery involving language – I suppose I mean jokes – was made into a fine art in Zen Buddhism. In an essay called *Wittgenstein and Zen*, Warren Shibles says of Zen's literary forms: 'The character and nature of the Koan and the Haiku are similar to Wittgenstein's writings also in that contexts and concepts are combined which are not usually associated with one another. . . . The humor involved is . . . a kind of therapy which reveals where we go wrong.'[33]

No wonder the Mahāyāna seems harder to understand than the Hīnayāna, and Wittgenstein harder to understand than Russell! A different kind of understanding is called for. If one tries to understand all that is said by the Mahāyāna and Wittgenstein after the pattern of *confrontation*, one will be faced with near-insoluble difficulties. These have often been felt and expressed, and even though they can by no means be wholly accounted for by the mistake of expecting to be *presented* with ideas for understanding, they would certainly be eased if that mistake were avoided. It is treatment which is offered, not theories. That is why it is no part of the role of the 'liberator' to base what he says on a fixed body of knowledge all ready for presentation. Wittgenstein says: 'The philosopher is not a citizen of any community of ideas. That is what makes him a philosopher.'[34] Similarly, in the Prajñāpāramitā:

> *Subhuti*: Even so should a Bodhisattva stand and train himself. He should decide that 'as the Tathāgata does not stand anywhere, nor not stand, nor stand apart, nor not stand apart, so will I stand, ... well placed because without a place to stand on.' ... When he trains thus, he adjusts himself to perfect wisdom.[35]

Subhuti's audience – 75,006 gods – hoping for something to get their divine teeth into, for some object for their undersanding, complain,

> What the fairies talk and murmur, that we understand, though mumbled. What Subhuti has just told us, that we do not understand. Subhuti read their thoughts and said: There is nothing to understand, nothing at all to understand. For nothing in particular has been indicated, nothing in particular has been explained.[36]

(Why not? – 'Since everything lies open to view there is nothing to explain.'[37])

Taking Nāgārjuna, for neatness, as a figurehead for the Prajñāpāramitā and the Mādhyamika, it must by now be clear that we ought not to worry about comparing 'Nāgārjuna the religious writer' with 'Wittgenstein the academic philosopher', because neither can be so narrowly labelled.

While Russell and the Hīnayāna *construct* a 'person' with some difficulty out of more real sense-data or dharmas, Wittgenstein and the Mahāyāna in general *start* with embodied people. So far is Wittgenstein from ignoring them that he is often accused of behaviourism (despite P.I. 307–8). People are not granted existence by analogy with ourselves; we do not have to 'work up to' the reality of people. Solipsism is only some suggested new uses for certain words which I want other people to accept. To avoid assuming the reality of people, one would have to set up doubts in the old revisionary metaphysics style. But it is not simply that people are presupposed in Wittgenstein's later philosophy as the communal users of language. People come in for more respect than they had received from Russell (and many others). This may reflect part of Wittgenstein's own personality. Certainly, a dilettante attitude to others' existence is very far from Wittgenstein's style, which seems rather earnest, lacking in frivolity and 'grown-up', especially by comparison with Russell's. The contrast is nicely illustrated in a remark of Ronald Jager's: '[Russell] did not hesitate for a moment to compare his definition of a number with his definition of a person. Russell found this comparison logically illuminating, and it is; Wittgenstein would have found it humanly scandalous, and it is.'[38]

The person-centred trend of the Mahāyāna can be traced back to the traditional account of the second Buddhist council, at which the Mahāsaṅghikas seceded from the Sthaviras. The former's name ('great assembly') refers to their wish for more widely-based assemblies. It is not known for certain whether they wanted non-arhats (those who had not attained Nirvāṇa) to be allowed to attend as well as arhats, or whether laymen as well as monks were to be admitted. But certainly, they represented a move towards greater lay involvement, as well as away from monastic strictness. Devotional attitudes were made acceptable. The Buddha, and now countless other Buddhas, were raised to a pinnacle of splendour which left arhats with a rather tame reputation. Arhats, to make matters worse, could be subject to temptations, ignorance and doubts and, more important, could be helped by others in their gaining of knowledge.

In the Mahāyāna, in fact, 'other people' even become the basis of the new goal of Bodhisattvahood. All else, even Buddhahood, is to be given up by Bodhisattvas for the sake of others. The Mahāyāna, says Conze, 'could count on much popular support for . . . its opinion that people are as important as "dharmas".'[39] And not only mundane people are important, but also 'celestial people' with much-discussed bodies of various kinds. The very possibility of salvation is now not only a matter of private effort. Without help from Bodhisattvas, enlightenment is not possible. It is fortunate that one can rely on their help.

The Meaning of 'I'

On the status of the 'self', or the meaning of the word 'I', Wittgenstein and the Mādhyamika have similar theories to react against. In both cases, what is rejected is the view of a person as a logical construction from simple particulars consisting of what we normally think of as presented to us (sensations, etc.) as well as a rather grudging acceptance of a bare subject. Russell began by thinking that acquaintance with the 'I' is probably possible, if only as marking the distinction between sense-datum and sensation. He came to believe, however, that perception was not relational, did not consist of objects presented to subjects at all.[40] The subject is not an entity with which we can be acquainted, but is thrust upon us by the needs of grammar.

Schayer has suggested that in a pre-canonical Buddhist tradition, the real existence of the 'person' (pudgala) was upheld. Whether or not this is so, it is certainly true that the Abhidharmists made a clear distinction between subject and objects (citta, caitta), and were, therefore, like the early Russell, able to distinguish between sense-datum and sensation. So whether or not we accept Schayer's idea, the Hīnayāna upheld a position on the self capable of generating a reaction. Stresses in the Hīnayāna position occurred because experience was analysed in terms of subject and object, yet in another sense there was no self to be aware of the objects. It is, admittedly, true that the function of the no-self (*anātman*) doctrine is not only to warn against the idea of an identifiable subject. The ātman which is rejected is that which is reborn, which acts and remembers, for instance, as well as that to which sense-data etc. are presented. But the fact remains that the doctrines of 'no-self' and of 'the subject' (or 'consciousness'; *citta*) fit together rather unhappily. Conze says: 'In using the word "consciousness", Buddhists try to speak in an impersonal manner of the fact that all my mental experiences happen to "me", are known to "me", are discerned by "me". In all references to "consciousness" the "I" is all the time in the background, though it must never be mentioned.'[41]

The Abhidharmists were trying to make satisfactory a theory which does have its attractions. The self is to be replaced by that of which we would usually say the self is aware. But it does not work. If there are to be genuine presentations, there must be someone to receive. Nāgārjuna cuts through the mistake: 'The self is not the experienced states, because they appear and vanish. How can "the experiencer" be "what is experienced"? Moreover, it does not obtain that the self is different from what is experienced. If the self were different, it would be perceived without what is experienced; but it is not so perceived.'[42]

Wittgenstein makes a point similar to the last-quoted verse. In Kenny's words: '*Having* toothache is not a relation between two terms, a person and a pain; for this to be so each term of the relation would have to be identifiable separately from the holding of the relation, which is obviously not the case.'[43]

The two following possible theories are rejected by Wittgenstein and the Mādhyamika: that there is a permanent self apart from what is experienced, and that there is only what is experienced, with no permanent self. The crucial point is that the term 'I' does not refer as a name at all:

Wittgenstein – 'The word 'I' does not mean the same as 'L.W.' even if I am L.W., nor does it mean the same as the expression 'the person who is now speaking'. But that doesn't mean: that 'L.W.' and 'I' mean different things. All it means is that these words are different instruments in our language.'[44] ' "I" is not the name of a person.'[45]

The Prajñāpāramitā – '*Subhuti*: I who do not find anything to correspond to the word "Bodhisattva", or to the words "perfect wisdom" – which Bodhisattva should I then instruct and admonish in which perfect wisdom?'[46] 'One speaks of "I" or "mine" or "I am" but no dharmic fact corresponds to this.'[47]

Once one thinks of 'I' as a name, one imagines that it must name either something or nothing. But, like the names of private sensations, it does neither. In fact, private sensations and the self are all part of the same picture, and they stand or fall together. The Hīnayāna had tried to deny the self while admitting real dharmas. The Mahāyāna say that this is only a partial view; the Hīnayāna idea that the self is not an object (pudgala-nairātmya) is to be replaced by the Mahāyānists' denial that any dharmas are objects (dharma-nairātmya). This change has always been seen as a completion of a limited viewpoint. Pudgala-nairātmya is not rejected: it is made coherent by discarding private sensations along with the self, or at least by denying them all the status of objects. *If*, on the other hand, one takes the possible items of experience to be objects to which names may refer, then one *must* allow the self in too. From the Blue Book:

> We feel then that in the cases in which 'I' is used as subject, we don't use it because we recognize a particular person by his bodily characteristics; and this creates the illusion that we use this word to refer to something bodiless, which, however, has its seat in our body.[48]

And, similarly:

> Candrakīrti complains that the Abhidharmikas have not given an adequate picture of the empirical even. 'If it is sought to depict the empirically real (vyavahāra-satyam) then besides momentary states, the activity and the agent too must be admitted.'[49]

For Wittgenstein, the statement 'I am in pain' is not *about* me at all. First-person statements of this kind are of a quite different sort from apparently similar third-person ones. When we make statements involving 'I' as subject, what we are saying is, as it were, too close to home to refer to anything.

> The difference between the propositions 'I have pain' and 'he has pain' is not that of 'L.W. has pain' and 'Smith has pain'. Rather it corresponds to the difference between moaning and saying that someone moans.[50]

> How does a human being learn the meaning of the names of sensations? – of the word 'pain' for example. Here is one possibility: words are connected with the primitive, the natural, expressions of sensation and used in their place.[51]

This is not behaviourism about oneself. Just as we need not 'look inside' to find out whether we have pains, hopes and so on, we need not look at our bodies either. A theory which suggested that we deduced that we were in pain (or hoped something) from evidence of any kind has clearly missed the point.

So it is no use puzzling over whether there is a 'self', or whether we can manage without it philosophically. The word 'I' doesn't refer at all. Existence versus non-existence doesn't come into it. Nāgārjuna says: 'There is the teaching of "the self" (ātma), and the teaching of "no-self" (anātma); but neither "the self" nor "no-self" whatever has been taught by the Buddha.'[52]

Strictly, this is not a new Mahāyāna claim. In the Hīnayāna scriptures, the Buddha declines to affirm or deny the existence of the self.[53] All that is said is that the self cannot be experienced. What Nāgārjuna is reacting against is the 'no-self' *doctrine* of the Abhidharmists: the idea that the self does not exist, but can be replaced by other objects. The only valid way of replacing it by separate objects is to make sure that one of the objects is a subject, a recipient for that of which one is aware. And that is what was meant to be avoided. The Mādhyamika reject as unsatisfactory the statements that the self exists and that it does not exist; but there is no objection to talking of 'I', 'person' etc. as long as it is realised that this is a matter of conventional truth. One can make use of such words, in the way we normally do, but we must not regard them as names for real objects with a mysterious and elusive nature. The self is *empty*. It has the same status as the private objects of which the self is imagined to be aware. It is only an 'illustrated turn of speech.'

Our view of the self is bound up with language in (at least) two ways; one obvious and one less so. The obvious way is that the idea of the self as a self-existent entity is linked to the syntactical requirement of a subject for verbs.[54] How can there be experiences if there is no one to have them? I say 'linked to' rather than 'the effect of' or 'the cause of' because it is far from clear (to me, anyway) that the influence has gone in one direction rather than in another. The less obvious way concerns the idea of the self being able, in using words, to stand apart from the rest of the world, including the private sensations presented to the self. Alan Watts has expressed it:

> Language *seems* to be a system of fixed terms standing over against the physical events to which they refer. That it is not so, appears in the impossibility of keeping a living language stable. Thinking and knowing seem to be confronting the world as an ego in the same way that words seem to stand over against events; the two illusions stand or fall together. Speaking and thinking are events in and of the physical world, but they are carried on *as if* they were outside it, as if they were an independent and fixed measure with which life could be compared. Hence the notion that the ego can interfere with

the world from outside, and can also separate things and events from one another.[55]

When it was suggested before[56] that private sensations neither exist nor don't in any satisfactory sense, it seemed necessary to offer reassurance that one's inner life had not been pumped dry. I would have thought that reassurance was even more necessary in the case of the self. For what could be more obvious and inescapable than that my experiences are, for me, on an altogether different footing from those of other people? You may be prepared to grant that neither sensations nor the self are separately identifiable entities, and even that it is possible to alter one's manner of coming to grips with the world so that one no longer interprets it in terms of I-it. Yet there *must*, you might well feel, be some sort of distinction (and it had better be a big sort!) between the immediacy of *my* experience and the assumed reality of everybody else's. Is this distinction being forgotten or 'drowned in theory' when the Mādhyamikas say that the self is empty, that it neither exists nor doesn't?

It is just here, I think, where the comparison with Wittgenstein is particularly fruitful. The organism and its environment are indeed mutually dependent; but that does not mean that I disappear into my surroundings. It is true that we should not think of everyone as objects corresponding to their names; but that does not mean that we have all lost equally and that I cannot distinguish myself from anybody else. That seems both frightening and absurd. Wittgenstein, however, helps us by pointing out that, although we can pick out the person referred to by 'he', 'she' etc., we cannot pick out the person referred to by 'I': 'The mouth which says "I" or the hand which is raised to indicate that it is I who wish to speak, or I who have toothache, does not thereby point to anything. . . . The man who cries out with pain, or says that he has pain, *doesn't choose the mouth which says it*.'[57]

It is true that there is a sense of loss about this, but there is a greater gain. The loss is the loss of reference for first-person statements; they seem a little *too* close to moaning and so on. But the gain (or one of them[58]) is that there can be no fear of being unable to distinguish myself from anybody else. My own 'point of view' of the world is *so* different, for me, from anyone else's that one could say that it's hardly a point of view at all. What other point of view could I have? For me, it isn't *a* point of view: it's either *the* point of view or *no* point of view (i.e. just the facts). The man who looks at the world doesn't choose the person who looks. The self disappears, then, because it is *so* obvious that it is *too* obvious to be of any use. To try to focus one's attention on it as an object is like trying to look at the edges of one's visual field. One would need somehow to stand outside oneself first.

Insight into the status (or non-status) of the self could, then, be expressed in quite different ways. One could stress the denial of the self as an object, while issuing warnings that, strictly, the self neither exists nor doesn't. This is what the Mādhyamika does. Another way, however, is to point out, while issuing those same warnings, that I cannot get outside my experience. This is not to reintroduce the subject to which external objects, private sensations and the like are presented. We have seen that the escape from this clear-cut subject–object view is not to a position where the word 'I' has no meaning at all, but to a position where it has a non-referential meaning such that the 'my-ness' of my experiences is so obvious that it is transparent, and cannot properly be compared with the 'your-ness' of yours. So this second approach puts the emphasis on the 'my-ness' of my experiences.

This is what the Yogācāra 'mind-only' (citta-mātra) doctrine does. For the Mādhyamikas, going beyond the subject-object dichotomy is expressed primarily in terms of 'emptiness': both subject and object are empty, and salvation consists in seeing them as empty. For the Yogācārins, the same thing is expressed primarily in psychological terms: an attempt is made to describe the 'state of mind' of someone who has attained liberation. This description too, of course, is meant to be salutory in that it helps others gain insight into what they have to achieve. Vasubandhu says:

> At that time there is a forsaking of the grasping at consciousness, and the yogin is established in the true nature of his own thought. . . . The absence of an object results also in the absence of a subject, and not merely in that of grasping. It is thus that there arises the cognition which is homogeneous, without object, indiscriminate and supramundane. The tendencies to treat object and subject as distinct entities are forsaken, and thought is established in just the true nature of one's own thought.[59]

That mind-only is one side of the coin whose other side is the Mādhyamikas' emptiness is suggested by the fact that such similar statements are made about both. Consider these sentences from the Lankāvatāra Sutra (italics mine):

> (Mind) is *beyond all philosophical views*, is *apart from discrimination*, is not attainable nor is it ever born: I say, there is nothing but Mind.
>
> Of neither existence nor non-existence do I speak, but of Mind-only, which has *nothing to do with existence or non-existence*, and which is thus free from intellection.

Suchness, *emptiness*, realm of truth, the various forms of the will-body – these I call Mind-only.[60]

When it is recognized that the visible word is no more than Mind itself, *external objects cease to be realities*, and there is *nothing but what is discriminated* by the mind and perceived (as external).[61]

Placing mind (citta) on the same level as Nirvāṇa in this way brings to a climax a tradition which had existed in all Hīnayāna schools, had been prominent in the Mahāsaṅghikas and emphasised even more in the Mahāyāna generally. I mean the idea that a certain kind of thought is always pure in its own nature; before contamination it is clear and translucent. Salvation is attained when this ever-shining consciousness is decontaminated and revealed for what it is. On the face of it, this accords pretty appallingly with the no-self doctrine and Conze, in one mood at least, regards the acceptance of both ideas as the 'combination of the uncombinable.'[62] I can only suggest that a Wittgensteinian interpretation of the no-self doctrine, or at any rate the Mahāyānist reworking of it, makes it less necessary to regard a considerable number of ancient Buddhists as having made fools of themselves. It also makes a good deal clearer the statements about the self neither existing nor not-existing.

Perhaps here someone will feel inclined to object that the way things really are cannot, according to Buddhism, be described in words, Wittgensteinian or otherwise. I do not claim, however, that Wittgenstein has described the 'true state of affairs' about the self. What he has done is shown how the word 'I' is used and is not used and how, because of this, there is nothing for the word 'I' to describe – though that is not to say that I cannot be described. If descriptions of selfhood or 'what it is like to be me' are wanted, one is being asked, presumably, to offer new theories which pin matters down more tightly than do the ordinary statements I make about myself. But once the mistake of treating the subject and its objects as distinct entities bearing names of their own has been pointed out, what positive statements can one make? One can only, I think, try to remind people of the fact that the self is unable to be lost as well as unable to be found, and that is what the Yogācāra did.

6 Two 'Mental Acts'

Volition

(a) *The Atomistic Account*

In my account of the atomistic plan of the world, as presented to us by Russell and the Abhidharmists, I did not say anything about their treatment of volition. It is obvious that they had to give some analysis of what it is to do something deliberately, because it is an inescapable feature of human life. It would be a very one-sided picture, one feels, if we were all claimed to be passive observers of everything that happens to us. For we *do* things too. There are voluntary actions as well as mere awarenesses of sense-data and mental states. Russell and the Abhidharmists admit this, but what they have to say about deliberate actions does not fit happily into their overall scheme, as we shall see.

Deliberate actions can be opposed to accidents (falling on a slippery floor), involuntary movements (breathing), things happening *to* one (being unexpectedly attacked), simple occurrences, even if to do with one's own body (the fact that my arm rises), and quite possibly several other things. But what all deliberate actions have in common, the atomists tell us, what sets them apart from all the others, is an essential ingredient – they are all preceded by a volition. Volition, according to this way of thinking, is the hallmark of *action*. Any movements my body may make, however much they may seem to be actions, or to be 'something I do', are not actions unless a volition comes first.

Surprisingly, however, we can become observers of our volitions, at least in principle. Willing is a mental state, according to Russell,[1] of which we can become aware by introspection; and volition (*cetanā*) is one of the mental states (saṃskāras) of the Abhidharmists, of which we can become aware as we watch the rise and fall of dharmas. It might well seem odd that we can be passive observers of something which is the very 'essence of action', but the only alternative on the atomists' premises would have been to allow the existence of a self which is not only aware of sense-data etc., but is also an agent, an essential doer. This might remove the necessity for our being aware of an experience of deliberateness, since it could be argued that the self cannot be aware of itself, but only at the cost of making a big hole in the atomistic scheme. It was bad enough to have to have a self at all, in the guise of a receiving subject, but if the essence of deliberateness was something of which we could become aware, at least the self would not also take on executive powers.

So if we can manage without an irreducible agent, and can make do with volitions, what does the analysis of deliberate action look like? What one might expect is that actions would be *caused* by volitions. A volition would *make* something happen – it would *force* an event into existence. That is, after all, how one thinks of deliberate action in one's own case. It isn't something one notices, it's something one does. Both Russell and the Abhidharmists, however, reject this idea because it involves an anthropomorphic view of causality. Their rejection of anthropomorphic causality extends to all cases of causality, not only to volition, but is particularly important in the case of volition because if anthropomorphism can be avoided there, it can be avoided anywhere. For the anthropomorphic view – that causes *compel* effects – arises from the illicit extension of the picture of an agent or a volition compelling a certain action.

What this false view is replaced by is an explanation in terms of functional dependence. To say that X causes Y is really to say that Y is a function of X – that we could in principle give a rule or formula according to which changes in the state of Y can be related to changes in the state of X. Unfortunately, Russell and the Abhidharmists continue to believe in volitions as separate entities, and they consider it possible to give them a respectable job to do, even though they were the paradigm of anthropomorphic causality. Let us start with Russell:

> A volition 'operates' when what it wills takes place; but nothing can operate except a volition. The belief that causes 'operate' results from assimilating them, consciously or unconsciously, to volitions. . . . It may be objected to the above definition of a volition 'operating' that it only operates when it 'causes' what it wills, not when it merely happens to be followed by what it wills. This certainly represents the usual view of what is meant by a volition 'operating', but as it involves the very view of causation which we are engaged in combating, it is not open to us as a definition. We may say that a volition 'operates' when there is some law in virtue of which a similar volition in rather similar circumstances will usually be followed by what it wills.[2]

Stcherbatsky in more than one place explicitly compares Russell's opinions on causality with the Hīnayāna doctrine of dependent co-origination (pratītya-samutpāda). Speaking of 'the doctrine of causality in the Hīnayāna', he says:

> Causation was called dependently-co-ordinated-origination . . . or

dependent existence. The meaning of it was that every momentary entity sprang into existence, or flashed up, in co-ordination with other moments. Its formula was 'if there is this, there appears that'. ... Strictly speaking, it was no causality at all, no question of one thing *producing* the other.... This notion [of] a law of co-ordination between point instants is not quite a stranger to modern science and philosophy. Cf. B. Russell, *On the Notion of Cause.*[3]

Elsewhere he speaks of 'an almost exact coincidence between Buddhist views [on causality] and the views recently expressed by Mr Russell.'[4]

The doctrine of dependent co-origination was held to account for the appearance and disappearance of dharmas. Some explanation of the fact that dharmas 'come and go' is required, and we are told that a conditioned dharma arises dependent on (or as a function of) other conditioned dharmas. They are all conditioned and conditioning. Volition is, of course, a conditioned dharma and is related to other dharmas by the formula of dependent co-origination. As with Russell, although volition remains only a shadow of its former 'compelling' self, there is still a tendency to give it a little power and hope it will keep quiet:

It wills (cetayati), thus it is volition (cetanā); it collects, is the meaning. Its characteristic is the state of willing. Its function is to accumulate. It is manifested as co-ordinating. It accomplishes its own and others' functions, as a senior pupil, a head carpenter etc. do. But it is evident when it occurs in the marshalling (driving) of associated states [dharmas] in connection with urgent work, remembering and so on.[5]

For Russell, even though there is no 'compelling' causality, 'nothing can operate except a volition.' For the Abhidharmists, even though it is the case that dharmas cannot force other dharmas into existence, being able to serve only as conditions, volition 'is evident in the marshalling of other dharmas.' Such inconsistency is inevitable if volition is kept as a separate mental entity. If volition as a dharma or mental state cannot *do* anything in an anthropomorphic sense, there is no point in allowing its existence at all. We can explain the dharma or mental state *hope* as the essence of all hopings, as what all instances of hoping have in common, as what the word 'hope' really means, and as something we can experience if we are careful. And we could give an explanation of the same kind for *volition*, except that a volition is not something which happens to occur. In esssentialist terms, it is the essence of action.

Russell was heir to centuries of Western thinking along such lines. Of course, he rejected the usual idea of a causal chain (in the old sense) being traceable back through overt action to a hidden volition, but he still assumes that there is such a thing as a volition which is what all deliberate actions have in common.[6] And in the Hīnayāna, a famous definition of action (karma) is that 'action is volition': 'It is volition (cetanā), O monks, that I call action (karma). Having willed, one acts through body, speech or mind.'[7]

So if we were to remove from volition the power to compel something, it could no longer serve its purpose of being the essence of all action, what all actions have in common, and what the word 'action' really means. The incompatibility is between, on the one hand, taking volition as the essence of genuine anthropomorphic causality, and, on the other, the repudiation of anthropomorphic causality altogether. This could be avoided in various ways. One could argue anthropomorphic causality to be generally applicable after all. One could argue that there is no anthropomorphic causality at all, not even in the case of action, such that one couldn't *make* anything happen. Or one could refuse to admit volition as an entity or essence of any kind, and consequently reject any causal relation between a volition and the action which follows it. This last is the line taken by Wittgenstein and the Mādhyamika.

(b) *The Account of their Critics*

Volition goes the way of all private sensations, and I need not repeat the basic arguments against them. But both Nāgārjuna and Wittgenstein have specific things to say about volition, which are worth looking at.

Nāgārjuna sets out the Hīnayāna view, ready for refutation: 'The most perceptive seer (Buddha) has said that there is action (*karma*) as volition and as a result of having willed. The variety of acts of that (action) has been explained in many ways.

Thus, that action which is called "volition": that is considered (by tradition) as mental; But that action which is a result of having willed: that is considered (by tradition) as physical or verbal.'[8]

The criticism of this Hīnayāna viewpoint forms part of a wider criticism of Hīnayāna theories of causality. Murti has indicated[9] that the two main possibilities considered for criticism by the Mādhyamika are identity of cause and effect and non-identity of cause and effect. The latter is the Hīnayāna view. Dharmas are quite separate from each other, even though they are mutually conditioned. Volition is one dharma, and those 'driven on' by volition are other dharmas. But we cannot validly regard volition as a cause of anything separate from itself. This is so if we take 'cause' in an anthropomorphic sense: 'If a product is produced in the aggregate of causes and conditions and does not exist in the aggregate, how will it be produced in the aggregate?'[10] 'If the product is *not* in the aggregate of causes and conditions, then the causes and conditions would be the same as non-causes and non-conditions.'[11] – or if we take 'cause' in a non-anthropomorphic, Hīnayānistic way. Here the argument is that if X is a condition of Y – that is, if Y is a function of X – the problems associated with anthropomorphic causality are indeed avoided. But now nothing can ever happen. When Y occurs, we can say that it occurred with X as a condition, or in functional dependence on X. Before Y occurred, however, we cannot relate it in any such way to X. Conditions are of use, it seems, only when no longer required:

'Certainly those things are called 'conditioning causes' whereby something originates after having come upon them;

As long as something has not originated, why are they not so long "*non*-conditioning causes"?'[12]

This is much the same argument as the one employed by Ryle in a critique (cast in a mould similar to Wittgenstein's), of a mechanistic view of volition. Billiard balls, he says,[13] 'cause' each other's movements, in a 'functional dependence' sense. Given the weight, movement etc. of one ball we can deduce the movement of the one it strikes. But we are *not* 'given' the movement of the first ball until someone has pushed it. And how it will be pushed is not predictable according to *any* formula. We cannot actually use our formulae for the functional dependence of one ball's movements on that of another until someone acts. Otherwise everything would be static. To parody Nāgārjuna:

'Certainly we can use our formulae of functional dependence when something happens in accordance with them;

But as long as nothing has happened, why not call them "formulae of functional *non*-dependence"?'

In more than one place, Wittgenstein argues against the idea of volitions as mental states or mental acts representing the deliberateness in voluntary actions, as something separate from the action itself. For instance:

> I deliberate whether to lift a certain heavyish weight, decide to do it, I then apply my force to it and lift it.... One takes one's ideas, and one's language, about volition from this kind of example and thinks that they must apply – if not in such an obvious way – to all cases which one can properly call cases of willing.[14]

'There is a difference between the voluntary act of getting out of bed and the involuntary rising of my arm. But there is not one common difference between so-called voluntary acts and involuntary ones viz. the presence or absence of one element, the "act of volition".'[15]

So of course the assumption that we can, with care, pick out a volition preceding every action is an illusion:

'In many cases of voluntary speech I don't feel an effort, much that I say voluntarily is not premeditated, and I don't know of any acts of intention preceding it.'[16]

'When I raise my arm "voluntarily" I do not use any instrument to bring the movement about. My wish is not such an instrument either.'[17]

In the section immediately following the latter quotation, Wittgenstein looks briefly at the other possibility mentioned above; namely, that 'cause' and 'effect' are identical, that a voluntary action can in no way be divided into volition and action:

> 'Willing, if it is not to be a sort of wishing, must be the action itself. It cannot be allowed to stop anywhere short of the action.' If it is the action, then it is so in the ordinary sense of the word; so it is speaking, writing, walking, lifting a thing, imagining something. But it is also trying, attempting, making an effort, – to speak, to write, to lift a thing, to imagine something etc.[18]

It will not do for Nāgārjuna either: 'If there were a oneness of the cause and product, then there would be an identity of the originator and what is originated.'[19]

If, then, we take 'cause', 'effect' or 'volition' as names for things, we find ourselves faced with a paradox reminiscent of the 'neither something nor nothing' one. Volition as a cause of action separate from the action itself is not feasible, nor is volition as identical to the action. The escapes from both paradoxes are similar. The language we use about volition is satisfactory in itself, as long as we don't try to force it into the role of naming private objects. What more can one do than distinguish voluntary actions from involuntary ones? – 'There is not one common difference . . . the "act of volition".'[20]

Nāgārjuna emphasises that if we are to be able to make use of our *ordinary* ideas of cause, effect, action etc., we cannot take the words to refer to separate entities. To reinterpret functional dependence as emptiness, as he does, is not to say that there is really no causation, no functional dependence, no action etc. It is to bring the ideas of cause, effect and action back from the philosophy of object-listing to their ordinary uses, back to their original home:

'What *we* do is bring words back from their metaphysical to their everyday use.'[21]

'The "originating dependently" we call "emptiness"; This apprehension i.e. taking into account (all other things), is the understanding of the middle way.'[22] 'You deny all mundane and customary activities when you deny emptiness (in the sense of) dependent co-origination (*pratītya-samutpāda*).'[23] 'When emptiness "works", then everything in existence "works". If emptiness does *not* "work", then all existence does *not* "work".'[24]

But if we see 'an action' and the rest as real particulars – real in their 'own-being' – we are faced with insoluble problems about, for instance, how far back we must trace the 'causal chain' emanating in action.

'If you recognize real existence on account of the own-being of things, you perceive that there are uncaused and unconditioned things. You deny "what is to be produced", cause, the producer, the instrument of production, and the producing action, and the origination, destruction and "fruit".'[25]

'Why does the action not originate? Because it is without self-existence.'[26]

'If you deny emptiness, there would be action which is unactivated. There would be nothing whatever acted upon, and a producing action would be something not begun.'[27]

Few comparisons between Wittgenstein and Nāgārjuna could be more striking than this insistence that if we are to use words at all, we must put our trust in ordinary ways of talking about things. To see things as empty is the only way of avoiding revisionary metaphysics, or claims that new meanings must be given to words. It would not be difficult to make the mistake of casting Nāgārjuna in this revisionary role, since most philosophers, East and West, have played it. Nāgārjuna and Wittgenstein, by contrast, stand out as defending the 'mundane and customary' uses of words.

This is not quite the same as the Zen attitude to language. In Shibles' opinion, 'The attack on philosophy involves the following views by the adherents of Zen and by Wittgenstein . . . That ordinary language use and everyday situations should be our guide rather than philosophy.'[28] I think that this is a fairly accurate remark about Zen, but it is not true of Wittgenstein. He attacks certain ways of doing philosophy, but not philosophy *per se*. Both Wittgenstein and Nāgārjuna, unlike Zen adherents, work within a recognisable philosophical framework of argument, refutation, etc., and have philosophical reasons for reliance on ordinary language. The realistic views of cause, effect etc. which Nāgārjuna rejects, are cast aside because they do not accord with the way we ordinarily think of and talk about cause and effect. One might take this merely as an example of Nāgārjuna's setting of one view against another, ultimately to destroy them all, and leaving only emptiness. But that is to ignore statements like: 'You deny all mundane and customary activities when you deny emptiness.'

Cause and effect are indeed empty, but that is not to say that it is a mistake to talk in terms of cause and effect. The case is just the same as talking of 'hope', 'I', or 'blue'. 'Conventional truth' is not 'conventional falsehood'. Wittgenstein says:

> When . . . we disapprove of the expressions of ordinary language (which are after all performing their office), we have got a picture in our heads which conflicts with the picture of our ordinary way of speaking. Whereas we are tempted to say that our way of speaking does not describe the facts as they really are. As if, for example the proposition 'he has pains' could be false in some other way than by that man's *not* having pains. As if the form of expression were saying something false even when the proposition *faute de mieux* asserted something true.[29]

This attitude towards the way we use words may also, incidentally, help to explain the apparently paradoxical formula which crops up so frequently in the *Diamond Sutra* (and elsewhere), and which tends not to be looked at too closely. An example is:

' "Wholesome dharmas, wholesome dharmas", Subhuti – yet as no-dharmas have they been taught by the Tathāgata. Therefore are they called "wholesome dharmas".'[30]

There are, in this short Prajñāpāramitā Sutra, over twenty instances of the formula, which is applied to a variety of things – dharmas, marks, arhats, personal existence, etc. In every case, we are introduced to the item (X), told it is a no-X and that therefore it is called 'X'. It is the last part which causes the trouble. One can understand that when, say, dharmas are mentioned, the reminder is given that (according to the Mahāyāna ontology), they are no-dharmas. But why does the Sutra go a step further to tell us that they *are* dharmas after all? The answer is that it doesn't. In all the examples of the formula, it is first said that the item in question is not an object, (i.e. it is a no-X) and *then* one is told that once it has been taught as a no-X, it may be called 'an X'. There need be no error involved in talking in terms of 'dharmas', 'cause', 'hope', or whatever, *once* one has realised that there are not objects corresponding to these terms. And in fact there is a passage near the end of the Sutra where there is an interesting addition to the formula. It runs:

> What was taught as 'seizing on a material object' by the Tathāgata, just as a no-seizing was that taught by the Tathāgata. Therefore is it called 'seizing on a material object.' – The Lord added: And also, Subhuti, that 'seizing on a material object' is a matter of linguistic convention, a verbal expression without factual content.[31]

This makes quite clear the fact that the expression in question has no objective reference, no 'factual content'; but is part of a language, a 'linguistic convention'. How else could one express 'seizing on a material object'? The only fault lies in false inferences from the fact that we use such a phrase.

Knowledge

I dealt above with the treatment by Russell and the Hīnayānists of perceptual knowledge, but the knowledge I am now going to consider is not of that kind. Your knowledge e.g. that $3+4=7$ or that one cannot score goals in cricket, cannot be reduced to sense-data. Knowledge of facts, knowledge that something is the case, seems so different from, say, the awareness of a red sense-datum, that one might expect different analyses of knowledge for each of the two cases. But this is not what we are offered. Once again[32] vision is the model – factual knowledge is the *confrontation* of the subject with what is known. Whatever is known is regarded as an object.

Jayatilleke has collected a considerable amount of evidence[33] from Pāli sources to show that knowing (jñāna) is based on the pattern of seeing. And non-perceptual knowledge, for the Abhidharmists, consists in the relation which obtains between the mind (mana-indriya-āyatana; the 'sixth sense') and the objects presented to it. Non-perceptual knowledge is made into a separate department, but it is on a level with, and of a kind similar to, the five sensual departments.

For Russell, too, knowledge of all kinds is relational. Facts can be known[34] either by means of acquaintance with the fact or by means of judgement. But both judgement and knowledge by acquaintance involve a subject/object scheme, with knowledge as involved in the relation between them. – 'We will call the mind the *subject* in the judgement and the remaining terms the *objects*.'[35] 'We spoke of the relation called "judging" ... as knitting together ... the subject and the objects.'[36]

And for acquaintance: 'Now I wish to preserve the dualism of subject and object ... Hence I prefer the word *acquaintance*, because it emphasizes the need of a subject which is acquainted.... The word *acquaintance* is designed to emphasize ... the relational character of the fact with which we are concerned.'[37]

According to Russell, then, we should look for knowledge of facts in the relation obtaining between the subject and that of which it is aware. One can, of course, know things outside the mind – sense-data, facts etc. – but the knowing itself is a *mental act*: 'There is on the one hand the thing of which we are aware ... and on the other hand the actual awareness itself, the mental act of apprehending the thing.'[38]

There is no inconsistency in holding knowing to be both a relation and a mental act – something the mind *does* – since, as Russell often points out,[39] verbs tend to express relations. What *is* a problem, however, is how, when knowledge is reduced to immediate acquaintance, one can know something when it is not 'before the mind'. I have known that $3+4=7$ since I was quite young, but I am not continuously thinking about it. Am I still acquainted with this fact during the gaps? Russell has this to say: 'As in most cognitive words, it is natural to say that I am acquainted with an object even at moments when it is not actually before my mind, provided it has been before my mind, and will be again whenever the occasion arises.'[40] Neither here nor anywhere else does Russell give any satisfactory account of how the gaps are bridged; but at all events, knowledge is not limited to the present moment.

Nor was it for the Sarvāstivādins. One of the arguments for their 'three times' theory[41] was that if dharmas were instantaneous, knowledge would be limited to the present, to those dharmas with which I am now acquainted. Like Russell, they seem to think of what is going on during the gaps as a sort of *survival* of an object which has been before the mind once and may be again. Knowing must have *something* to do with the confrontation of a subject and an object which is known; so if at three o'clock I knew that $3+4=7$, but didn't think about it, it must be that the confrontation took place in the past and still has the potential to recur.

This, however, is one of the weak points of a relational view of knowledge, and it is dealt with at some length by Wittgenstein. He gives the example of an order to continue a series of numbers by adding 2. If the pupil makes a mistake, and writes 1000, 1004, 1008, one would know it to be wrong:

> 'But I already knew, at the time when I gave the order, that he ought to write 1002 after 1000.' – Certainly; and you can also say that you *meant* it then; only you should not let yourself be misled by the grammar of the words 'know' and 'mean'. For you don't want to say that you thought of the step from 1000 to 1002 at that time – and even if you did think of this step, still you did not think of other ones.[42]

So one can know something without ever having thought of it. This suggests that knowing need not have anything to do with the mind, the knowing subject, at all. Still less, then, could knowing be a mental act. Of a case where the order is 'add 1' (not 'add 2', as above), Wittgenstein says:

> 'Surely I knew when I gave him the rule that I meant him to follow

> up 100 by 101.'... Was knowing this some mental act by which you at the time made the transition from 100 to 101, i.e. some act like saying to yourself 'I want him to write 101 after 100'? In this case ask yourself how many such acts you performed when you gave him the rule.[43]

It is no use expecting Wittgenstein to tell us what knowledge really is, since he says it isn't a mental act. Any such essentialist definition of it will run into difficulties. Suppose an exact definition of the word 'knowledge' is asked for:

> As the problem is put, it seems that there is something wrong with the ordinary use of the word 'knowledge'. It appears we don't know what it means, and that therefore, perhaps, we have no right to use it. We should reply: 'There is no one exact usage of the word "knowledge"; but we can make up several such usages, which will more or less agree with the ways the word is actually used.'[44]

But even though all such attempted definitions of knowledge are doomed to create trouble, the definitions involving mistakes most worth pointing out are those which are the most common. So Wittgenstein spends a good deal of time showing the problems involved in regarding knowledge as a mental act or as a relation between subject and object, between a mind and what it knows.

How did the Mādhyamika react to the Abhidharmists' view of knowledge as relational? It can be summed up in Robinson's words (paraphrasing Hui-Yüan): 'According to the *Great Perfection of Wisdom Treatise*, the ultimate principle is that there are no real objects corresponding to ideas or words, that cognition is not a relation between real objects and real perceivers.'[45]

For Nāgārjuna, non-perceptual knowledge goes the way of the five kinds of perceptual knowledge. The subject–object model is rejected, as one would expect in view of the fact that, as we have already seen, the Mādhyamika accept neither a real subject nor real objects for it. 'If there is no "seer", how can there be vision and the object seen?'[46] ... '(Likewise) hearing, smelling, tasting, touching *and thought* are explained as vision. Indeed, one should not apprehend the "hearer", "what is heard" etc. (as self-existent entities).'[47] (My italics).

The same attitude is expressed by Seng-Chao, a Chinese Mādhyamika. In a work of his, translated by Robinson as *Prajñā has no Knowing*, he argues that the Holy Man has knowledge, but realises that there are no 'objects of knowledge'. For brevity, I shall again quote Robinson's summary of the translation. Seng-Chao is replying to objections:

OBJECTION: The Sage knows and acts, so you are wrong in denying him these functions.

REPLY: What I actually said was that he knows without apprehending objects.[48]

OBJECTION: Since Prajñā has the Absolute Truth for its object, it is wrong to say that Prajñā has no object, and thus wrong to say that Prajñā has no knowing.

REPLY: Prajñā has no knowing precisely because it knows the Absolute Truth, which is not an object.[49]

OBJECTION: If Prajñā does not apprehend, then either it does not apprehend because it has no knowing, or it knows first and then does not apprehend. Thus the Holy One either is totally blind, or his knowing is distinct from his not apprehending.

REPLY: Both alternatives are wrong. His knowing is identical with his not apprehending, and so he can know while not apprehending.[50]

The Sage, then, is not denied the ability to know, but 'he knows without apprehending objects.' 'Wisdom (prajñā) . . . is a cognition (jñāna) without an (objective) sphere.'[51] In Dignāga's words: 'Prajñāpāramitā is non-dual knowledge (jñānam advayam).'[52] But of course it would be a mistake to think of this 'non-dual knowledge', or knowledge without a subject–object dichotomy, as a special possession of the Sage. As we shall be discovering in the next chapter, there can be no difference in content between what is known by an ordinary, unenlightened person and what is known by someone with 'perfect wisdom', who sees everything as empty. As Streng points out: 'The assertion of some independent reality "behind" the expression of knowledge would preclude any knowledge of emptiness.'[53] To see things as empty is partly to realise that knowledge is not something my mind does with objects. The point is *not* that there are two kinds of knowledge – relational for the ordinary person, and non-relational for the enlightened. There is no relational knowledge: some don't realise this and some do. The Mādhyamikas and Wittgenstein both offer a new way of looking at the knowledge we have had for all these years: in short, they both hold that neither 'knowledge' nor knowledge requires an object. 'Knowledge' (the term) does not require to correspond to it an object such as a mental act. And knowledge does not require an object in which 'what is known' is hypostatised. So to imagine that there are either two kinds of knowledge (on the model of two kinds of mental act) or two different kinds of object of knowledge would obviously be no more than two kinds of mistake. They are mistakes rather unlikely to arise from reading Wittgenstein, but worth warning against in the case of the Mādhyamikas – although perhaps the lack of any sort of objects of knowledge should be obvious enough when we remember the fact that there are no real dharmas to 'get into view'. The avoidance of both mistakes is summed up in this extract from the *Perfection of Wisdom in Eight Thousand Lines*:

> *The Lord*: The perfection of wisdom does not procure any dharma, and in consequence of that fact she comes to be styled 'perfection of wisdom'.
>
> *Sakra*: Then, O Lord, this perfection of wisdom does not even procure all-knowledge?
>
> *The Lord*: It does not procure it as if it were a basis, or a mental process, or a volitional act.
>
> *Sakra*: How then does it procure?
>
> *The Lord*: In so far as it does not procure, to that extent it procures.[54]

7 Ethics and Religion

Ethics

Neither Russell nor Wittgenstein (after the Tractatus) spent much time on philosophical ethics. In this section, therefore, the parallels will be less personal although, I hope, no less valid. For Russell, I shall more or less substitute G. E. Moore, whose ethical theories are closely tied to a referential theory of meaning. And in the *Elements of Ethics*, Russell adopted Moore's views that goodness is an indefinable quality which cannot be demonstrated, that one can make mistakes in identifying it, and that a right action is one leading to the most goodness. For Wittgenstein I shall not need to substitute anyone in particular, though I shall be partly concerned, as many moral philosophers have been since, say, the second world war, with the metaethical implications of later Wittgensteinian ideas.

In his preface to *Principia Ethica*, Moore tells us that he has carefully distinguished and attempted to answer two questions. 'What kind of things ought to exist for their own sakes?' and 'What kind of actions ought we to perform?'[1] I realise that *Principia Ethica* seems, if it is possible, even further removed from Hīnayāna Buddhism than do the works of Russell, and it is true that many of Moore's conclusions differ greatly from Buddhist ones. It happens, however, that in looking at what answers Moore gave to his two questions and at what answers the Abhidharmists would have given, we find that there is a common pattern; and that the common pattern is related to the similarities already noted between the Abhidharmists and Russell.

'What kind of things ought to exist for their own sakes?' Moore's answer was that it seemed quite obvious to him that personal affection and the contemplation of beauty were of much more value than anything else, even if they existed by themselves. That, according to Moore, is the crucial test. We can discover what is of intrinsic value only if we consider what would be of value even when entirely alone. Further, no evidence can be given for a thing's being of intrinsic value. If the thing was good for some *reason*, its goodness would lie in the reason, not in itself.

The Abhidharmists' answer to Moore's first question is 'Nirvāṇa'. Nirvāṇa, unlike all conditioned dharmas, is a dharma worthy of attainment in itself; it is the goal to which the 'Way' leads. And it is referred to as *paramattha* or *uttamattha*, both meaning 'the highest good', 'of supreme import'. One might translate them as 'intrinsic good'. No reasons can be given for the intrinsic value of Nirvāṇa.[2] It might be thought, for instance, that it can be commended as a prime example of peacefulness or pleasure. But arguments from the value of things in the conditioned world to the value of those in the unconditioned are not found in Buddhist texts. And, in the Hīnayāna, there is a vast gulf between Nirvāṇa and everything else, so that nothing else is properly commensurable with Nirvāṇa. 'No reasons can be given for doing this [sc. attaining Nirvāṇa]; it is its own justification. To do it is to leap into the light of a practical *revelatio*.'[3]

What is uniquely worth aiming at, according to Moore and the Abhidharmists, has simply to be *seen* as being of value. Yet the respective ideals are thought of as 'good' or 'the best' in an objective sense. If Moore is right about friendship and beauty, and the early Buddhists about Nirvāṇa, then other people are making *incorrect* statements if they disagree. What is the best really *is* the best, regardless of anyone's opinions. What is intrinsically good is not a matter of taste, but a matter of fact.

Moore's second question was 'What kind of actions ought we to perform?' His answer was, briefly, that we ought to perform those actions which bring about the greatest balance of good over evil. Ideally, of course, we are aiming at the two Mooreian intrinsic goods. In the Hīnayāna, actions and certain mental states are commended in so far as they conduce towards Nirvāṇa. The only things regarded as worthwhile are, first, Nirvāṇa, the intrinsically valuable dharma, and, second, what can lead to it. We saw above[4] that the Abhidharmists hypostatised or 'dharmified' goodness and even allowed Nirvāṇa to be evaluated as 'sukha'. The tendency common here to Moore and the Abhidharmists is based again on the assumption that to mean is to refer. Evaluative words have meaning, so must refer to identifiable objects – Moore's 'good', or the Abhidharmists' 'sukha' or 'goodness of behaviour'.

It is perhaps worth pointing out here that there is a mistake very commonly made about Buddhist ethics. Although Nirvāṇa is the prime goal, it is *not* the case that an action is morally good in Buddhism in so far as it tends to bring about the attainment of Nirvāṇa. This can easily be seen by considering that the training necessary for enlightenment is separated into three parts: morality, meditation and wisdom (sīla, samādhi and prajñā). In the nineteenth century, Hīnayāna Buddhism was commonly seen in the West as nothing but a great big system of teleological ethics. That phase has now passed, but has, unfortunately, been largely replaced by a view of Buddhist *ethics* which makes 'conduciveness to Nirvāṇa' the moral criterion.[5] Since meditation and wisdom are also conducive to Nirvāṇa, this suggests that they too are morally good, thus blurring the distinction between the three 'trainings'. I have suggested elsewhere[6] that it is best to think in terms of a two-tier evaluation system here. There is higher-order evaluation which rates Nirvāṇa as intrinsically good and commends the three trainings, including morality as a whole, as good because they lead to the goal. But there is also a lower-order, or moral, evaluation concerned, unlike meditation and wisdom, with what one morally ought to do.

I think that this two-tier system is a useful scheme of interpretation, first because it makes it clear that Buddhism, unlike Moore, does not hold that everything tending to the ideal goal *ought* to be done. It is no moral fault not to practise meditation, for instance. It is also useful because it allows one to express the fact that in the Hīnayāna morality is (*relatively*) unimportant. Higher-order evaluation belittles morality not simply by evaluating it – 'morality as a whole is useful for attaining Nirvāṇa' – but by giving it third place out of three. Wisdom is the most directly useful for enlightenment, but is assisted by meditation, and that in turn by morality.[7] Similarly, 'purity of morality is of purpose as far as purity of mind'[8] and so on through seven stages up to Nirvāṇa; and each stage derives its importance from its conduciveness to the next. Morality, then, has the least importance – it is only preparatory. It is referred to as 'the trifling matters, the minor details, of mere morality'.[9]

Morality is regarded as, in a way, even less than preparatory. One must *get past* the stage of attachment to doing what one 'ought' at the very outset:

> Hence let a man renounce all rule and rite
> And all the acts that draw down blame or praise.
> Long not for 'cleansing' won from this or that,
> Fare free of such, accepting not that 'calm'.[10]

Before morality is purified – while, that is, one is concerned with what one 'ought' to do – perfection in morality will be one's goal. But if one is to have Nirvāṇa as one's goal, this stage must be passed:

> But once his morality is perfected
> His mind then seeks no other kind
> Than the perfection of Nirvāṇa
> The state where utter peace prevails.[11]

There are similes, too, linking the aspirant's 'dependence' on morality to dependence on prior removal of physical obstructions. For instance:

'As, sire, a tumbler, who wants to show his craft has the ground dug, the grit and gravel removed and the ground made level, and then shows his craft on soft ground – even so, sire, does the earnest student of yoga, depending on morality, and based on morality, develop the five controlling faculties etc.'[12]

Let me sum up the similarities between Moore's views on ethics and those of the Abhidharma. The quality of moral goodness is made into an *object* existing independently of people's opinions. It has a similar status to private sensations or dharmas. The 'object' is discovered by means of the same kind of essentialist thinking which we saw to operate for 'hope' and the rest. All examples of moral goodness have something in common underlying all valid uses of the words 'morally good', and this something can be experienced: Moore would say that we knew goodness by intuition, the Abhidharmists that we were aware of the dharmas corresponding to the phrase 'moral goodness'.

For both of them, the value of all valuable things can be traced to either one or two objects of irreducible value. Everything else can be valuable, worthwhile, good, etc., only if it tends to bring about the intrinsically good – friendship and contemplation of beauty for Moore, Nirvāṇa for the Abhidharmists. There is the difference, however, that we are told by Moore that everything which leads to the ideal objects ought, in a moral sense, to be done; but the Abhidharmists say that although it is good (in a 'higher-order evaluation' sense) to do what leads to Nirvāṇa, moral 'oughtness' applies only to part of the Way.

Since morality has in some sense been 'left behind' by the Arhat, the Hīnayāna can say that to have attained Nirvāṇa is beyond good and evil. The Arhat, specifically, is beyond merit and demerit derived from karma (puñña and pāpa).[13] And Nirvāṇa itself is argued by the Theravāda to be not morally good since it has none of the attributes necessary to what is 'karmically meritorious'.[14] For the Hīnayāna, this getting beyond good and evil is a real attainment. Moral goodness and badness are objectively real and so is Nirvāṇa. The enlightened person is, crudely, someone who has left behind association with the one to take up association with the other. In moral, 'lower-order evaluation' terms, there is not much that can be said about such a change. But in 'higher-order evaluation' terms, such a person is decidedly better-off.

We would not, of course, expect the Mādhyamika to be satisfied with such a picture. What they have to say here is what is to be expected. All statements about morality and evaluation are matters of conventional truth. Nirvāṇa is no better an object than is Saṁsāra. The enlightened person is not objectively better-off at all. It is true that the Perfection of Morality is one of the Six Perfections, part of the Bodhisattva's career. But 'through the fact that neither self nor being nor morality nor enlightenment have been apprehended, he cleanses the perfection of morality for the sake of enlightenment.'[15]

The most obvious way of putting it is to say that according to conventional truth, morality is real, and that according to absolute truth, it is not. Matics, for instance, expresses just such a point of view, and says: 'On the plane of moral duty, one sees himself sinful and the other virtuous; but from the plateau of near-Enlightenment, that high elevation which reveals the identity of Nirvāṇa and Saṁsāra, there is a poetic sense wherein reality is bliss, but a truer, philosophical sense in which value judgements do not apply.'[16]

I do not say that this is mistaken, exactly. It seems to me that it is just as informative and just as misleading as to say, of the Mādhyamika-Wittgensteinian epistemological outlook, that 'dharmas/private sensations do not exist'. It would be all right for Matics to say that 'value judgements do not *refer*', but not that 'value judgements are not *valid*', which is what I suppose him to mean. On the lack of a reference for moral terms, we are back to familiar ground. 'Goodness' and the like no more express (non-physical) qualities than do sensation-words. Wittgenstein says:

> Or suppose someone says, 'One of the ethical systems must be the right one – or nearer to the right one.' Well, suppose I say Christian ethics is the right one. Then I am making a judgement of value. It amounts to *adopting* Christian ethics. It is not like saying that one of these physical theories must be the right one. The way in which some reality corresponds – or conflicts – with a physical theory has no counterpart here.[17]

To say, with the Mādhyamika, that moral evaluations belong only to conventional truth is not to say that there are really no moral evaluations, but to say that, although there are evaluations, they are not something 'underlying' what we say in our use of moral terms. Ethical language-games, like all others, are 'complete'[18] in that we cannot say something extra about ethics by trying to step outside that language-game. To investigate morality as deeply as possible brings one not to the 'essence' of goodness etc. but to the way in which ethical words are used:

> What *makes* the word ['good'] an interjection of approval? It is the game it appears in, not the form of words. (If I had to say what is the main mistake made by philosophers of the present generation,

including Moore, I would say that it is when language is looked at, what is looked at is a form of words and not the use made of the form of words.)[19]

In the case of private sensations, we saw that it was reasonable to say that 'there is a difference between pain-behaviour with and without pain', but that we must avoid the danger of thereby creating inner objects. In the case of the self, we saw that it was reasonable to make first-person statements, but that we must avoid the danger of assuming that the self is an entity of some kind. And now, in the case of morality, and evaluation more generally, the position is similar. First, there is nothing the matter with statements involving moral and other evaluational terms. Wittgenstein's attitude, of course, is that the way moral terms are used is satisfactory in itself. If we try to improve on such uses, we alter what was originally said. The Mādhyamika attitude is that what we can say (in conventional truth) about morality is satisfactory: goodness and badness are hardly the same. Nothing could be more obvious than that a Bodhisattva's compassionate attitude is better than someone else's cruel one. The millions of acts of Mahāyāna devotion towards Buddhas and Bodhisattvas leave no room for the possibility that they are really to be thought of as no better than anyone else. Even the most hard-headed Mādhyamika texts generally begin or end with devotional salutations. So it is certainly not the case that evaluative statements are all mistaken, all the outcome of a wrong-headed way of viewing things.

Secondly, there is a danger to be avoided. Basically, it is the assumption that moral terms refer to objective qualities. I have already quoted Wittgenstein on this, and the Mahāyāna is equally keen to reject the idea that there can be any objective or factual difference underlying the difference between a good thing and a bad one. The potential Bodhisattva must not make the mistake of looking forward to moral superiority or to possessing a 'quality' of goodness, though that is not to say that morality is not important.

'He does not settle down in views about morality as his refuge; because perfect purity of morality does not result from taking refuge in views on morality.'[20]

> Nor do Bodhisattvas who course in the objective supports of giving or meanness, morality or immorality, course in the perfection of wisdom. And why? Because they have fully comprehended the objective supports of giving or meanness, morality or immorality, and in that comprehension of their objective supports there is no coursing; therefore is the coursing of a Bodhisattva called a no-coursing.[21]

And what of the positive evaluation – the glories! – of perfect wisdom, emptiness etc.? Emptiness is indeed a superior viewpoint from the angle of conventional truth. But, once it is seen according to absolute truth, there is no object called 'emptiness' to be thought of as superior, nor any other objects to be rated as good or bad. It is a conventional truth (not a falsehood) to say that Nirvāṇa is better than Saṁsāra; but once we start trying to focus on 'betterness', we start to veer away from emptiness again. Let me quote a Prajñāpāramitā passage which sums up a great deal:

> *Mañjuśrī*: That, O Lord, is a development of perfect wisdom when one approaches neither the faults of birth-and-death (Saṁsāra) nor the virtues of Nirvāṇa. For one does not review birth-and-death, how much less its faults! And I do not apprehend Nirvāṇa, how much less can I see its virtues! . . . One does not think that these dharmas are superior and that those dharmas are inferior, and one also does not apprehend the dharmas which might be superior or inferior. . . . The development of perfect wisdom, O Lord, does not imagine any dharma as superior or inferior. There is nothing superior or inferior about non-production, or about Suchness, the Reality limit or all the dharmas. Such a development, O Lord, is a development of perfect wisdom.
>
> *The Lord*: Are then again, Mañjuśrī, the Buddhadharmas not supreme?
>
> *Mañjuśrī*: They are supreme (agrā), but just because they cannot be seized upon (a-grāhyatvād). Has again, O Lord, the Tathāgata fully known all dharmas to be empty?
>
> *The Lord*: So he has Mañjuśrī.
>
> *Mañjuśrī*: But one cannot, O Lord, conceive of superiority or inferiority in emptiness?
>
> *The Lord*: Well said, Mañjuśrī, well said! So it is, Mañjuśrī, as you say![22]

The Abhidharmists had believed that Saṁsāric, conditioned dharmas are impure or defiled, while Nirvāṇa is beyond all faults and therefore undefiled, untainted or pure. Now, however, we are told that defilement and purification are not 'objective qualities' at all: 'Even defilement is markless, how much more so purification! Defilement and purification, both these dharmas are markless and without total reality.'[23]

If Nirvāṇa is a real attainment, as the Hīnayāna says it is, it is difficult to avoid desiring it, even though the scriptures naturally warn against this. Nirvāṇa's objective superiority over Saṁsāra means that before one attains it, one is worse off in a very real way – after all, the distinction between defilement and purification, or between the conditioned and the unconditioned, is a dharmic, that is, a factual difference. It is a *fact* that it is *better* that Nirvāṇa should take over from conditioned dharmas. All this, it seems to me, makes for stress. When the Hīnayānist is having the wrong kind of thoughts, is being tempted by un-Buddhistic ideals, is wicked or doesn't practise meditation often enough, he is (measurably) going the *wrong* way. Karmic demerit piles up hideously. The best thing, then, is to wrench oneself from worldly temptations and become one of the monks, who alone, according to a strong Hīnayāna tradition, can attain Nirvāṇa. How could one expect it to be easy to kick out mundane dharmas in favour of supra-mundane?

In the Mahāyāna, all this is changed. There is no factual difference between Saṁsāra and Nirvāṇa, and so neither guilt about demerit nor gritting of the teeth in general. And according to absolute truth, there is no difference between absolute and conventional truth,[24] so that even though 'one speaks of the "supramundane" as that which has completely transcended all verbal concepts, . . . the supramundane is not a matter of rising above, but a matter of not rising above . . . And why? In relation to it even the least dharma does not exist which one should rise above.'[25]

It is very tempting, in certain moods, to wish to set oneself on the right track by looking for a fixed ideal to live up to. 'If only this mood (or attitude, or emotion . . .) that I'm in now could become dominant in me. I would "rise above" the worst in myself.' One wishes to force a certain mood or ideal into the role of overriding or perhaps somehow justifying other moods and ideals. Sadly, this rarely seems to work. There are so many other mood-claimants, some of them so intense. Perhaps I made the wrong choice!

The Mahāyāna tendency is to allow them *all* in, because they can all be transformed by being seen as empty. There are no special 'Nirvāṇic facts' to lean towards – all facts partake of Suchness and are the basis of enlightenment. Enlightenment, then, is open to all, not only to a select group. Naturally, this must seem to the Hīnayāna to be laxity and wishful-thinking. Even at the secession of the Mahāsaṅghikas, the orthodox (Sthavira) attitude was mistrust at the idea of giving Buddhism a wider base. But the Mahāsaṇghikas made monasticism both less rule-bound and less doctrinally necessary, and the Mahāyāna moves in the same direction. The really important change, however, is not the granting of the chance of salvation to all people, but offering the chance of a part in salvation to all one's 'mental contents'. Seeing them as they really are – as empty – is what is called for, not (higher-order-) evaluating them as inferior to something yet to be attained.

Religion
I suggested in Chapter 5 that we need not worry about comparing Nāgārjuna the religious writer with Wittgenstein the academic, because they have enough in common to override these descriptions. Here, I start by assuming that the worry has not gone away and offer another way of appeasing it.

Buddhism is, after all, a religion, and Wittgensteinianism, despite some hero-worship, tendencies towards belief in scriptural infallibility and so on, is not. But Wittgenstein expressed certain views of religion and of which interpretations of 'religious belief' and 'religious truth' are reasonable and which not. His attitude is summed up by Pears:

> A religious tenet is not a factual hypothesis, but something which affects our thoughts and actions in a different way. This sort of view of religion fits very naturally into his later philosophy: the meaning of a religious proposition is not a function of what would have to be the case if it were true, but a function of the difference that it makes to the lives of those who maintain it.[26]

In his lectures on religious belief, for instance, Wittgenstein said:

> Suppose somebody made this guidance for his life: believing in the Last Judgment. Whenever he does anything, this is before his mind. In a way, how are we to know whether to say he believes this will happen or not?
>
> Asking him is not enough. He will probably say he has proof. But he has what you might call an unshakeable belief. It will show, not by reasoning or by appeal to ordinary grounds for belief, but rather by regulating for all in his life.[27]

Statements of what is believed in a religious way are not, then, to be taken as statements about historical or other empirical facts. A sentence like 'There will be a Last Judgement' expresses a certain attitude to life. If one does not have this attitude, there is not much one can say about the Last Judgement.

> Why shouldn't one form of life culminate in an utterance of belief in a Last Judgment? But I couldn't say either 'Yes' or 'No' to the statement that there will be such a thing. Nor 'Perhaps' nor 'I'm not sure'. It is a statement which may not allow of any such answer. . . . If an atheist says, 'There won't be a Judgment Day', and another person says there will. do they mean the same? – Not clear what

criterion of meaning the same is. They might describe the same things. You might say, this already shows that they mean the same.[28]

In a case like the Last Judgement and Wittgenstein's remarks about it, we are faced with a familiar situation. There are certain statements from within Christianity which are seized upon by philosophers of religion, who tell us what kinds of statements they are. The statement from within Buddhism which centrally concerns us, however, is 'All dharmas are empty'. Here, there is no need for philosophers of religion to set to work, because the Mādhyamika has already done the job for us. It has its own built-in philosophy of religion. There is, as we have seen, *no* factual difference between absolute and conventional truth, or between Nirvāṇa and Saṁsāra. The advantages of absolute over conventional truth, or of Nirvāṇa over Saṁsāra, are not advantages of correctness or validity so much as advantages stemming from a better attitude to life. One is transformed, not by grasping at last the 'Ultimate fact about the universe', but by realising that facts are not 'hard': 'Since all visible and ideal entities are regarded as empty of self-sufficiency, there can be no universally valid ultimate human experience. There is, however, according to Nāgārjuna, a universally valid means for avoiding all claims to ultimacy, and this is the awareness of their emptiness.'[29]

'All dharmas are empty' certainly does not express any kind of *commitment*, as does a Wittgensteinian view of 'There will be a Judgement Day' – at least in part. What the two statements have in common is that there need be no factual disagreement between people who would make such statements and those who wouldn't. In the Christian example, the people in question would be a 'believer' and an 'unbeliever'. In the Buddhist example, the people would be 'someone who is enlightened, who sees things as empty' and 'someone who doesn't'. This is no doubt an important distinction between the two religions, (inseparable from a welter of other differences), but that does not affect my main point; which is that, according to Wittgenstein and according to the Mādhyamika, religious assertions correspond not to any matter of fact, but rather, roughly, to a certain attitude to life. Streng, as usual, makes it quite clear:

The awareness of 'emptiness' is not a blank loss of consciousness, an inanimate empty space; rather it is the cognition of daily life without the attachment to it. It is an awareness of distinct entities, of the self, of 'good' and 'bad' and other practical determinations; but it is aware of these as empty structures. Wisdom is not to be equated with mystical ecstasy; it is, rather, the joy of freedom in everyday existence.[30]

How different Wittgenstein is here from Russell, and how different the Mādhyamikas from the Abhidharmists! It is no good, according to Russell, saying that religion is 'useful' rather than 'true'. Religious tenets must be judged by their truth or falsity, and that means whether or not they correspond to the facts. To say that 'God exists' is not to say something about human life, but is a factual claim. And Nirvāṇa became, under the Midas fingers of the Abhidharmists, a valuable, glittering object to be sought after – but still an object, an existent.

Another idea about the non-factual nature of religious belief or faith, one frequently associated with the 'attitude to life' view, is that things or events can be experienced in a religious way, yet the same things or events can also be experienced in a non-religious way.

John Hick, for instance, starts from Wittgenstein's discussion of puzzle-pictures at P.I. II xi. These are ambiguous diagrams, such as the drawing of a cube viewed from below to one viewed from above. Hick compares the two 'aspects' of such a drawing with the experience of a religious and of a non-religious person. Naturally, he extends the *visual* ambiguity of the pictures to *all* the senses for this purpose, and then applies this 'experiencing-as' not only to drawings but to real life. 'And the analogy to be explored is with two contrasting ways of experiencing the events of our lives and of human history, on the one hand as purely natural events and on the other hand as mediating the presence and activity of God.'[31]

The debt to Wittgenstein, in fact, extends further than Wittgenstein's discussion of puzzle-pictures. Not only does Wittgenstein himself want to change our way of 'looking at things'[32] or our 'way of seeing':[33] he also considers, in his discussion of the differences between religious belief and non-belief, a case in which someone who is ill wonders what the 'retribution' is for. His point is that someone who thinks in this way accepts the same facts of the matter as someone who doesn't think in terms of retribution.

'Take two people, one of whom talks of his behaviour and of what happens to him in terms of retribution, the other one does not. These people think entirely differently. Yet, so far, you can't say they believe different things.'[34]

If I don't think of illness as punishment at all, it's not that I believe 'the opposite' to the one who does: 'I think differently, in a different way. I say different things to myself. I have different pictures.'[35]

And Wittgenstein then goes on to express parallel views about belief/disbelief in a Judgement Day.

For people like Hick, then, religion is emptied of factual content in the sense that the difference between a religious and a non-religious person lies in identical facts being experienced differently, like cube-'pops'. This obviously fits very well the idea that Nirvāṇa and Saṁsāra are not different. It is also, of course, closely related to the point made above: that someone who asserts that 'all dharmas are empty' is not making a factual assertion but expressing something like an attitude to life. The point being made *now* is that he is expressing an attitude to the same things and events towards which everyone else has some attitude or other. He experiences the same things and events which everyone else experiences, but they are 'experienced-as' empty. There is no factual difference between experiencing the world as real dharmas and experiencing it as empty. As Streng said: 'the awareness of "emptiness" ... is an awareness of distinct entities ... but it is aware of these as empty structures.'[36] And the Perfection of Wisdom says:

> The perfection of wisdom cannot be expounded or learned ... by means of the skandhas, elements or sense-fields [i.e. by classifications of dharmas] because all dharmas are isolated, absolutely isolated. Nor can the perfection of wisdom be understood otherwise than by the skandhas, elements or sense-fields. For just the very skandhas, elements and sense-fields are empty, isolated and calmly quiet. It is thus that the perfection of wisdom and the skandhas, elements and sense-fields are not two nor divided.[37]

But, you might feel, if there is no factual difference between A and B (the same facts being 'experienced-as' A and B respectively), isn't there liable to be some difficulty in explaining how to recognise A's and B's? This problem is very real for Hick. If an event can be 'experienced-as' a natural event *or* as an act of God, we need to know how to recognise natural events and acts of God. And we need to know what is the difference between them, if there is to be any use in talking in terms of 'acts of God' (or, for that matter, 'natural events') at all. Hick mentions this difficulty. To experience the ambiguous cube drawing as, say, a cube seen from above, we need first to have had acquaintance with cubes seen from above. So how can we experience an event as an act of God without *prior* acquaintance with acts of God? When we ask to see an act of God, we are shown only an event which *can* be experienced-as an act of God.

Hick's defence is that there is no such thing as raw experiencing. All experiencing is experiencing-as *something*. If we see a fork we recognise it *as* a fork. Or perhaps we make a mistake and see it *as* something else. A Stone-Age savage would fail to recognise it at all because he would see it *as* 'a small but deadly weapon; or as a tool for digging; or just as something utterly baffling and unidentifiable.'[38] And since, according to Hick, all experiencing is experiencing-as, and also since we can successfully recognise, say, forks, we must at some time have learned to recognise forks. Similarly, he says, we can 'learn to use the concept "act of God", as we have learned to use other concepts, and acquire the capacity to recognise exemplifying instances.'[39]

This, it seems to me, is mistaken. There is no difficulty in recognising exemplifying instances of forks: they can be pointed out quite straightforwardly. But to see an 'act of God' is, in Hick's view, to see 'an event experienced-as an act of God'. It is impossible to break this vicious circle, and impossible to point unambiguously to an 'act of God', even after one has acquired the alleged skill of recognising them as such. This, notice, does not hold for 'natural event', (the alternative way of experiencing events experienceable-as acts of God), even though natural events cannot be pointed out like forks. For we can understand how to recognise a 'natural event' by having our attention drawn to certain regularities and patterns in the events of the world. To recognise a natural event is to experience an event as linked in with these regularities and patterns in a certain way. But what comparable way could there be of recognising an act of God as such? It is all very well to say that we can come to recognise God's activity in the world, but we need first to know what is involved in recognising an act of God. An explanation in terms of 'experiencing-as' doesn't in itself get us anywhere.

The question now is: what about emptiness? Experiencing things as empty has in common with experiencing events as acts of God the fact that nothing at all need be left over. To experience an object as a fork involves separating it from its surroundings, but in the case of emptiness and acts of God, it makes sense to talk of experiencing *everything* in these ways. So does the problem about prior understanding apply also to emptiness?

It is worth noticing first that the fact that *everything* can be experienced-as empty is not in itself a problem, because *all events* can be experienced-as natural events without any difficulty about prior understanding of the meaning of 'natural event'. Yet obviously we cannot explain the meaning of 'emptiness' by pointing out regularities or, apparently, by making any remarks about the world. What we *can* do, however, is explain emptiness by talking about language, as I have already indicated. When we try to explain 'natural event', we can remain inside the world because the explanation does not require us to go further. And when we try to explain 'emptiness', there is again no need to step outside the world, invoking the Absolute perhaps, because the explanation is in terms of the way people use words. We can learn to recognise things as empty by learning about how words can have meaning without referring. Hope, for example, can be experienced-as a private object or experienced-as empty. It is useless to talk of it as experienced-as empty unless we can explain what 'empty' means in this case. We can. What it means is that 'hope' does not have meaning by referring to anything.

All this is not to say that there is an objective world waiting to be experienced-as empty or otherwise, like a neutral duck-rabbit picture waiting to be experienced-as a duck or a rabbit.

We can validly distinguish the colour-range (the spectrum) as objective from our colour-classifications as subjective. We can say that people employing different colour classifications *see* the world *as* being different because of that, even though they are *seeing* the same objective world. But we need to remember that the very distinction between 'neutral objective world' and 'classified subjective world' is itself a distinction we have drawn. There *is* an objective world, just as blue *is* a colour, precisely because that is how we talk of things.

Pears says that objectivism collapses into anthropocentrism.[40] Here we see the other direction of the 'oscillation'. Anthropocentrism turns into an objectivism because it allows us to say that there *is* an objective world. We *can* say that there is an objective something which can be experienced either as empty or as a private object, but we go astray if we fail to realise that this 'objective something' is itself empty – itself a result of our having distinguished a 'neutral, objective something' from the same thing 'experienced-as' x or y. There really is a neutral objective world (not yet experienced-as anything in particular), just as there really is hope – not as what is referred to by the terms 'neutral objective world' or 'hope', but simply as what the terms mean.

Yet since the 'neutral objective world' is itself empty, the choice between experiencing hope as a private object or as empty is a false one, since there is no neutral material for experiencing-as anything. And, conversely, there *is* neutral material because there is an objective world, because we can distinguish it from a 'subjective world'.

This ought not to make one reel. It is the 'oscillation' Pears mentioned, which has also been called a 'dialectical balance'. Philosophy of this kind is in a deliberately unstable equilibrium, and cannot, therefore, have any static theories, as we already knew.

A discussion about the religious aspects of any part of the Mahāyāna – not least the Prajñāpāramitā – would be incomplete without mentioning what may well seem to some the most obvious 'religious' tendency of all in Buddhism. I mean the greater emphasis in the Mahāyāna on worship and devotion, to which attention has already been drawn. There are whole devotional schools in Mahāyāna Buddhism, but I am more concerned here with instances of devotion in Prajñāpāramitā or Mādhyamika texts. This is because it is in these texts, I think, where one could reasonably least expect to find devotional writing. The main originality and thrust of the Prajñāpāramitā and the Mādhyamika has little or nothing to do with devotion at all. In many Mādhyamika works admittedly, reverential attitudes are hardly found, but in Prajñāpāramitā texts, devotional passages abound and, most important, have a typically Mahāyāna flavour. That is, by, say, Sarvāstivāda standards, the expressions of devotion are *excessive*. Apparently, then, the Mahāyānist tendency towards increased devotion was felt to be quite compatible with the other main strands in Prajñāpāramitā thought with which we have been dealing.

One of the most striking facts about devotion in the Prajñāpāramitā is that the reverence held to be due to people or things in certain passages seems somewhat diluted by statements in other passages to the effect that those people or things do not really exist. Let us look at some examples. The main objects of devotion are, on the one hand, Buddhas and Bodhisattvas, and on the other, the Perfection of Wisdom itself. Of the Buddha, for instance, we read:

> Thereupon the Lord at that time smiled a golden smile. Its lustre irradiated endless and boundless world systems, it rose up to the Brahma-world, returned from there, circulated three times round the Lord, and disappeared again into the head of the Lord. When she saw that smile, that woman seized golden flowers, and scattered them over the Lord. Without being fixed anywhere, they remained suspended in the air.[41]

And of the Perfection of Wisdom:

> The perfection of wisdom gives light, O Lord. I pay homage to the perfection of wisdom! She is worthy of homage. She is unstained, the entire world cannot stain her.[42]

Yet there is also:

> All objective facts also are like a magical illusion, like a dream. The various classes of saints, from Streamwinners to Buddhahood, also are like a magical illusion, like a dream.[43]

> I who do not find anything to correspond to the word 'Bodhisattva' or to the words 'perfect wisdom', – which Bodhisattva should I then instruct and admonish in which perfect wisdom?[44]

What we find, then, is devotion without objects of devotion. But how, in that case, are we to take the devotional passages? Presumably references to a golden smile and golden flowers are not to be understood as factual assertions? That is so, in the sense that it would show a misunderstanding of the passage to question a botanist on the likelihood of golden flowers remaining suspended in the air; but that is not to say that the passage needs to be rewritten. There may be no better way of saying what the passage says. Wittgenstein says:

'"We might see one another after death" . . . isn't the same as saying "I'm very fond of you" – and it may not be the same as saying anything else. It says what it says. Why should you be able to substitute anything else?'[45]

To ask for a backing up of the passage with scientific evidence is to misapply the picture which is being used. It is like, in an example of Wittgenstein's, talking of eyebrows over the Eye of God. One must not, however, assume that a picture is simply the contingent expression of a certain feeling or attitude. It is easy, for instance, to imagine the statement that 'the Perfection of Wisdom is the mother of all the Buddhas' to be, not a literal statement of family relationships, but, therefore, a way of expressing a certain feeling of reverence towards the Perfection of Wisdom. But that simply won't do. One couldn't put 'I think the Perfection of Wisdom is marvellous' in its place. Yet if the original statement only expressed an attitude (as expressed in the second one), lots of different pictures would do to express it. Wittgenstein says:

'"He could just as well have said so and so" – this (remark) is foreshadowed by the word "attitude". He couldn't just as well have said something else. If I say he used a picture, I don't want to say anything he himself wouldn't say.'[46]

So when we come to consider the fact that most Hīnayānists (and especially Abhidharmists) would not have wanted to use a picture like 'The Perfection of Wisdom is the mother of all the Buddhas', we must beware of saying simply that the Mahāyānists had a more devotional attitude, although this would not be false. More to the point, they found themselves able to use these new pictures. There was a greater freedom to employ gorgeous and often extravagant pictures which would have been regarded by the Hīnayāna old guard as out of the question. I cannot possibly discuss all the reasons there may have been for this enlargement of devotional pictures in the Mahāyāna; but what I do want to consider is the relation it bears to the changes and developments from Hīnayāna to Mahāyāna to which attention has been paid so far in this book.

Let me start by pointing out, as many have done before me, that the use of a certain picture, like, in our case, 'The Perfection of Wisdom is the mother of all the Buddhas', involves appropriate 'criteria of intelligibility' or 'criteria of rationality'. What this means is that there are some extensions of the picture, such as 'The Perfection of Wisdom is the mother of all the Bodhisattvas', which would not be out of place or absurd; and others, such as 'Is the Perfection of Wisdom married?', which would. The criteria of rationality associated with a certain picture fix the boundary of sensible questions and extensions. If, for instance, only descriptive statements about what concretely exists are regarded as respectable, any religious pictures which are used will be severely limited by that narrow criterion of rationality. And that, of course, is just what we find in the Hīnayāna. It is reasonable to believe something if there is evidence to back it up. This ties up with the stress on descriptive language which I have mentioned before. Nāgārjuna, however, says:

'Those who describe in detail the Buddha, who is unchanging and beyond all detailed description – those, completely defeated by description, do not perceive the Tathāgata.'[47]

In the Hīnayāna, one could be 'defeated by description' only perhaps in the case of Nirvāṇa, which is said to *atakkāvacara*, 'not in the realm of logical thought'.[48] But the general attitude is summed up by Jayatilleke: 'Early Buddhism should therefore be regarded not as a system of metaphysics but as a verifiable hypothesis discovered by the Buddha in the course of his 'trial and error' experimentation with different ways of life.'[49] He quotes Warder approvingly: Buddhism 'sought knowledge . . . which we may characterize as scientific on account of its basis of *perception*, *inference*, *verification*, etc.'[50] (italics Jayatilleke's).

Now, when contrasted with this hard-headed approach, the Mahāyāna may well seem plagued with irrationalism, and this charge has often been made. But to call the Mahāyāna pictures irrational is to judge them by alien, perhaps Hīnayānist, standards of rationality. What makes the Mahāyāna pictures possible – philosophically possible, if you like – is the wider view that is taken of language. The restricted, 'description-only', approach to language, the consequent narrow criteria of rationality and the limitations to the use of pictures which were *its* consequence; these were the positions the Mahāyāna left behind. And so their philosophical and devotional innovations are not at all unconnected. A wider view of how language works enables more to be said: the Mahāyāna said more.

8 Disconnection and Connection

In this last chapter I shall be looking first at the most important way in which Wittgenstein and the Mahāyāna are *not* related, and then at some important ways in which they *are*. A list of all the ways in which two people or things are unrelated would obviously be endless and largely trivial: only where there might be a temptation to argue for a link is there any point in showing that the link does not really exist. So the only link which I am concerned to show as illusory is one which, if it *could* be established, would be a philosophical bombshell: the notion, that is, that some of Wittgenstein's ideas could have been derived, even if indirectly, from the Mahāyāna. Proof of such influence would, of course, invalidate much of what I have written, since I have been assuming that the similarities need to be accounted for in a quite different way.

Buddhism, Schopenhauer and Wittgenstein

What makes the idea of Wittgenstein having been influenced by the Mahāyāna seem at least plausible is the fact that Arthur Schopenhauer is one of the few Western philosophers who have been influenced by Buddhism, and is also one of the few philosophers known to have influenced Wittgenstein. On the first point, Patrick Gardiner, in his book on Schopenhauer, says:

'He pointed out on a number of occasions . . . that . . . there were many . . . ways in which his philosophical conclusions broadly corresponded to cardinal conceptions implicit both in the mystical texts that make up the Upanishads and in Buddhist scriptures (particularly, it would appear, those of the Mahāyāna school).'[1] Conze goes so far as to say that 'the degree of affinity existing between Schopenhauer and Buddhism will give us a standard by which to judge other alleged parallels.'[2] Schopenhauer's thought, he says, 'partly under Indian influence, exhibits numerous, and almost miraculous, coincidences with the basic tenets of Buddhist philosophy.'[3] I agree with Conze that Schopenhauer was probably influenced by his reading about Hinduism and Buddhism, and consequently I cannot agree that the coincidences are 'almost miraculous'. It is true that Schopenhauer himself said:

> If I were to take the results of my philosophy as the standard of truth, I would be obliged to concede to Buddhism the pre-eminence

> over the rest. In any case it must be a satisfaction to me to see my teaching in such close agreement with a religion which the majority of men upon the earth hold as their own . . . This agreement must be the more satisfactory to me because in my philosophizing I have certainly not been under its influence.[4]

It is difficult, however, to take this quite literally, if only because he often explains his ideas with the help of Buddhist terms, especially 'Nirvāṇa', which he takes, in keeping with contemporary views, to mean a kind of extinction.[5]

On the extent to which Wittgenstein was influenced by Schopenhauer, a great deal could be said. It is generally accepted that the later parts of the Tractatus bear such influence, particularly those parts dealing with ethics, religion and 'the will'. The only kind of influence which is really of interest to us, however, is that which might form a link between Wittgenstein and Buddhism. And the only relevant connection that I can find is that Schopenhauer

> drew attention (however indirectly) to the way in which, even in their everyday employment, concepts relating to 'the will' – such, for instance, as wanting, intending, trying and choosing – have a far greater complexity than has always been assumed by philosophers. To imagine that their meaning can be given simply by pointing to various distinct 'interior' occurrences discernible by introspection is, at the very best, to accept a vastly over-simplified view of their functions in thought and language . . . [In this] he anticipated in noteworthy respects the philosophical challenge to the entire Cartesian approach – exemplified by the later writings of Wittgenstein and by the work of Gilbert Ryle – in the present century.[6]

But that is all. In general, we may be quite sure that Wittgenstein did not derive his later ideas from Buddhism via Schopenhauer, and for two reasons. First, the affinities between Schopenhauer and Buddhism[7] do not correspond at all with those that exist between Schopenhauer and Wittgenstein. Second, the similarities between Wittgenstein and Buddhism are far too detailed to have passed on via Schopenhauer, who, in denying influence by Buddhism, says that in 1818, when *The World as Will and Idea* was first published, there were very few good books on Buddhism. Judging by the bibliography of the 'best words on Buddhism', which he gives in his *On the Will in Nature*, in the section called *Sinology*,[8] one can only agree with him. None of the works which he mentions could possibly have given him much information about the Mādhyamika; and even *if* they had done so, none of it found its way into his books.

It seems that the only possible way in which Schopenhauer could have been instrumental in making Wittgenstein know the details of Mahāyāna Buddhism was by merely promoting in Wittgenstein an interest in Buddhism. For even that, however, there is no evidence whatever. So, unless I am completely mistaken, the close resemblances at which we have been looking can best be explained as being similar reactions to similar stimuli. They are not resemblances due to philosophical heredity. 'The author of the *Philosophical Investigations* has no ancestors in philosophy':[9] only predecessors.

Conclusions

Finally, I ought to say what I consider to have been established in the preceding chapters, so that if I am wrong I can be seen to be wrong. If I am right, of course, no summary can show me to be so: only the piecemeal arguments can do that.

First, I think that a Wittgensteinian interpretation of Mahāyāna Buddhism, and especially the Mādhyamika, clarifies a lot of apparently separate issues. The Mahāyānists may not have been such irrationalists and lovers of paradox as they are often thought to have been. In particular, I think that useful light has been shed on several long-standing issues, of which the following are probably the most important:

(a) Various statements about dharmas: that they are indistinguishable, that they neither exist nor don't, that they are empty and isolated.

(b) Emptiness in general: it has nothing to do with Kantian Absolute. Statements about emptiness are statements about how words are used. For the same reason, emptiness does not imply nihilism.

(c) Well-known contradictions: why there is 'no difference' between Nirvāṇa and Saṁsāra, and between absolute and conventional truth.

(d) The self: both the Abhidharmist *anātman* doctrine and the criticism of it by the Mahāyāna.

(e) The emphasis on language: and those words to which we are told that nothing corresponds.

Secondly, as to Wittgenstein, comparison with the Mahāyāna puts emphasis on some points which have not been accustomed to it. But at the end of the day I have only one new thing to say about him, around which everything else revolves. It is this: much of what the later Wittgenstein had to say was anticipated about 1800 years ago in India. I hope that by now it will be clear that this claim is not based on a strained interpretation of a few verses of scripture. I have tried to show that substantial parallels can be traced because the same movement of thought occurred for broadly the same reasons. The similarities between Wittgenstein and the Mahāyāna would be less impressive if they could not be shown to be similar reactions against similar views. Not only are the philosophical views of the Abhidharmists and Russell similar, they are in a way more strikingly similar than are those of the Mahāyāna and Wittgenstein. But that is not really surprising. Atomism starts from fairly simple, clear-cut premises, which almost inevitably lead to certain conclusions. Given the original fact that a certain kind of philosophical atomism sprang up in the East something like 2300 years ago, and in the West fifty to sixty years ago, there is nothing odd in being able to find detailed coincidences of theory. The Wittgensteinian–Mahāyānist way of reacting to these views is much less predictable in its details because, although there is an approach common to both (and indeed common to all the problems they deal with), it does not produce any theories, so that one can look for detailed equivalences only where the same subject is being dealt with.

That is why the greater part of this book has been divided up under different topic-headings. This is a rather unnatural way of going about things because, (as must have been obvious), the divisions between topics in this particular style of philosophising are more or less artificial. It was possible for the Mahāyānists to deal with different subjects in an organic way, often returning from various directions to deal with the same point; quite different from the neat chapter-headings of the Abhidharmists.[10] It was possible too for the *Philosophical Investigations* to have been written as a solid piece, without hard and fast divisions between the problems dealt with. But of course it is impossible to point out the links between two great wholes without breaking them down into smaller parts.

Does it matter that Wittgenstein's originality has been impaired? As it happens, it matters a good deal less than it would in the case of most other philosophers. According to Wittgenstein himself, it is not important if one's philosophical thoughts have been thought before. What matters is that they should do their job of liberating one from perplexity and that one knows oneself to be better off in some way. If other people a long time ago solved similar problems in a similar way, there is no reason to despair. On the contrary, perhaps Wittgensteinians should take heart from the long-standing philosophical reputation of the Mādhyamikas.

I do not say, of course, that Wittgenstein's ideas and those of Mādhyamika Buddhism are identical and interchangeable. I have argued that we should not too lightly assume that there are irreconcilable differences between a religion and a philosophy; but there do remain differences, though *outside* the sphere of the comparisons which have been made. This is because a religion is more than its doctrines – more than what it says. A complete description of the Mādhyamika would have to include mention of the monastic order, rituals, devotional writing and belief in celestial Bodhisattvas, all of which it involves and none of which are relevant to Wittgenstein. The reason why these elements do not spoil the comparisons is that they are logically separable from writings about emptiness etc.; except, of course, that the latter may make for greater possibilities in the use of devotional language, for instance, as we have seen. The point I am making is that all the religious elements I mentioned could have been entirely different or perhaps even non-existent without this having had any influence on the Mādhyamikas' religio-philosophical doctrines. *Historically*, the two are for ever linked: *logically*, they are (with the above reservation) contingent. The historical fact means that we cannot say that Wittgensteinianism and the Mādhyamika are 'just the same'; all modern adherents of the Mādhyamika ought, in my submission, to be Wittgensteinians, but followers of Wittgenstein need not become Buddhists. The logical fact means that any samenesses which can be found are genuine samenesses and remain unsullied by other equally genuine differences.

It would, doubtless, be convenient if we could say that the philosophical aspects of the Mādhyamika contribute to these samenesses, and its religious aspects to the differences, but that is too simple. A good deal of what would universally be called 'religious' in Mādhyamika texts can also, I argued in Chapter 5, be found in Wittgenstein's work. I know it seems distasteful to be asked to recognise the kind of liberation, insight and change offered by Wittgenstein as having a 'religious quality'. The predominantly philosophical and intellectual Mādhyamika also seemed distasteful to many contemporary Mahāyānists for just the equivalent and opposite reason – it was not religious enough. Still, it will not really do to reclassify Wittgenstein's work under 'religion': librarians, relax. Let us only remember, then, that Wittgenstein offered benefits which most representatives of academic philosophy – towards which Wittgenstein expressed considerable antipathy – would find embarassing.

Notes

PREFACE

1 Conze: TYBS 229.
2 Ibid.

1 *Logic*

1 See Edgerton, vol. II, 276 (meanings (1) and (2)).
2 Stcherbatsky: CCB 26.
3 Jayatilleke s.485.
4 K.V. 335–8.
5 Jayatilleke s.501.
6 Conze: BTI 220 (citing P.f, 505b).
7 See Stcherbatsky: CCB 40, 42.
8 Ayer 55.
9 Stcherbatsky: BL. I, 142.
10 Russell: Probs 139.
11 Russell: Probs 140.
12 Guenther 35.
13 See Russell: Probs 201.
14 Jayatilleke s.596.
15 M. I, 403.
16 Schilpp 699.
17 Stcherbatsky: CCB 106.
18 VM. XIV, 155.
19 Ibid.
20 See e.g. Ryle 104–5.
21 E.g. VM. XVI, 56.
22 See PTSD 716.
23 A. IV, 414; Mil. 313.
24 VM. IV, 100.
25 VM. IV, 94–8.
26 VM. IV, 100.
27 VM. IV, 151–2.

2 *Experience and its Objects*

1 Russell: Probs 17.
2 Russell: M & L 150.
3 Stcherbatsky: CCB 55.
4 Russell: Probs 78.
5 Conze: BTI 110.
6 Russell: Probs 12.
7 Mundle 17.
8 Mundle 16.
9 VM. I, 54.
10 Russell: Ph.L.A. 129.
11 Russell: Ph.L.A. 134.
12 A.K. III, 15.
13 M. II, 263.
14 Russell: M & L 148–9.
15 Mundle 72.
16 Stcherbatsky: CCB 42.
17 A.K. V, 24.
18 Jayatilleke s.793.
19 Jayatilleke s.718.
20 Asl. 43 (cf. VM. XXII, 8–10).
21 VM. XIV, 7.
22 Russell: Probs 77.
23 Ibid.
24 See above p. 17f.
25 See above p. 15.
26 Johansson 51–2.
27 Ud. 80.
28 Guenther 32.
29 VM. XIV, 63.

3 *Sensations and Language*

1 Wittg: P.I. 293.
2 See e.g. Wittg: Z 469.
3 Wittg: P.I. 258.
4 Conze: BWB 66.
5 Conze: TYBS 77.
6 E.g. Conze: SPT 169.
7 Aṣṭa 348.
8 S.P. I, 119 (tr. Conze).
9 Aṣṭa 475.
10 Wittg: P.I. 294.
11 Aṣṭa 347.
12 Wittg: P.I. 295.
13 Robinson 49.

14 Wittg: P.I. 304.
15 V.P. 31b.
16 See e.g. Stcherbatsky: CBN 43 on Candrakīrti.
17 M. 1, 135.
18 V.P. 6.
19 Wittg: P.I. 270.
20 Wittg: P.I. 271.
21 Conze: SPT 149.
22 Conze: BTI 221.
23 Robinson 49.
24 Ibid.
25 MK 24:10.
26 Streng 139.
27 Wittg: P.I. 220.
28 Wittg: P.I. 569.
29 Wittg: P.I. 10.
30 Wittg: P.I. 304.
31 Wittg: BB 5.
32 Robinson 46.
33 Wittg: PESD 248.
34 Pears: W 132–3.
35 MK 5:1.
36 Suv. 39b.
37 Wittg: P.I. 304.
38 Wittg: P.I. 307.
39 Wittg: P.I. 305.
40 Wittg: PESD 254.
41 Wittg: P.I. 290.
42 Robinson 49 (citing 'Hundred Treatise', ch. 10, pp. 181c24–182a1).
43 Streng 142.
44 Wittg: BB 56.
45 Streng 39.
46 Aṣṭa 200.
47 Wittg: PESD 233.
48 MK 24:10.
49 Witt: P.I. 305–7.
50 Wittg: P.I. p. 174.
51 Wittg: TLP 6.522.
52 van Peursen 110.
53 Robinson 49.
54 P. 261.
55 MK 25:19–20.
56 Streng 45.
57 See Wittg: P.I. 241, p. 226.
58 Streng 69.
59 Feyerabend 449.
60 Robinson 43.
61 Wittg: P.I. 124.
62 Wittg: P.I. 599.
63 Wittg: P.I. 128.
64 Wittg: P.I. 109.
65 MK 13:8.
66 MKV 247–8 (tr. Murti 163).
67 VV 29.
68 Suv. 64b.
69 Wittg: P.I. 126.
70 Wittg: P.I. 129.
71 Madhyāntavibhāgaṭika, by Sthiramati, p. 50 (tr. Conze: BTI 205).
72 Wittg: P.I. 255.
73 Wittg: P.I. 133.
74 Kāśyapa-Parivarta, p. 97, sec. 65 (tr. Murti 164).
75 See above pp. 10–13.
76 MK 12:9.
77 MK 24: 21, 23.
78 Har-Dayal 159 (cited Conze: BTI 249, n.28).
79 MK 24:30.
80 MK 24:18.
81 MK 24:40.
82 See e.g. Wittg: P.I. 293.
83 Wittg: Z 487.
84 For discussion, see Pears: BR & BT 182.
85 See below pp. 92–3.
86 Aṣṭa 206.
87 Wittg: P.I. 154.
88 Wittg: P.I. 68–71.
89 Aṣṭa 46–7.
90 Ibid.
91 Murti, *passim*.
92 Pears: W 28.
93 Streng 76.
94 Murti 294.
95 Murti 352.
96 Murti 235.
97 Streng 169.
98 Streng 166.
99 Robinson 43.
100 Aṣṭa 439.
101 Streng 54.

102 Wittg: P.I. 47.
103 Wittg: P.I. 50.
104 Pears: W 170.
105 BCA IX, 35.

4 *Yogācāra Contributions*

1 Conze: BTI 251.
2 LS 104–5.
3 Wittg: P.I. 244.
4 LS 225.
5 LS 226.
6 LS 88.
7 E.g. LS 144
8 See above p. 37.
9 LS 155.
10 Wittg: BB 18.
11 LS 156.
12 LS 88.
13 Aṣṭa 441.
14 Stcherbatsky: BL I, 444.
15 Stcherbatsky: BL I, 445.
16 Vācaspatimiśra on Apoha-vāda (tr. Stcherbatsky: BL II, 406).
17 Wittg: BB 17.
18 See above p. 43 (d).
19 Bambrough 198–9.
20 Pears: W 132.
21 Wittg: BB 133–4.
22 Wittg: BB 134.
23 Wittg: BB 135.
24 Stcherbatsky: BL I, 146–7.
25 Stcherbatsky: BL I, 457.
26 Stcherbatsky: BL I, 458.
27 Stcherbatsky: BL II, 259.
28 Stcherbatsky: BL II, 263.
29 Ibid.
30 Stcherbatsky: BL II, 404.
31 Wittg: BB 108.
32 Wittg: P.I. 261.
33 Stcherbatsky: BL I, 464.
34 Streng 142.

5 *Others and Myself*

1 Streng 142.
2 Wittg: BB 35.
3 Murti 211.
4 See above p. 45 (h).
5 Streng 142.
6 Pitcher: PW 206.
7 See e.g. Janik and Toulmin 26.
8 Fann 104.
9 Fann 110.
10 Wittg: P.I. 115.
11 Wittg: P.I. 309.
12 Wittg: P.I. 109.
13 Wittg: BB 27.
14 Fann 104.
15 Murti 216.
16 Aṣṭa 15.
17 Pitcher: PW 327.
18 Wittg: P.I. 133.
19 Bartley 4 (citing Malcolm 39).
20 Malcolm 32.
21 Malcolm 28.
22 Bartley 71.
23 Streng 171.
24 See above pp. 47–9.
25 E.g. Russell: Probs 235.
26 M. I, 265.
27 Wittg: P.I. 87.
28 Wittg: P.I. 288.
29 Wittg: Z. 452.
30 Wittg: P.I. 133.
31 Wittg: LAPR 28.
32 Aṣṭa 75.
33 Shibles 96.
34 Wittg: Z 445.
35 Aṣṭa 37–8.
36 Aṣṭa 38.
37 Wittg: P.I. 126.
38 Jager 421.
39 Conze: TYBS 50.
40 Russell: A of M, 141–2.
41 Conze: BTI 110.
42 MK 27:6 (and see Murti 203).
43 Kenny 138 (referring to Wittg: PB 91).
44 Wittg: BB 67.
45 Wittg: P.I. 410.
46 Aṣṭa 7.
47 Suv. 16b.
48 Wittg: BB 69.
49 Murti 249.
50 Wittg: BB 68.
51 Wittg: P.I. 244.
52 MK 18:6.

53 S. IV.400
54 See Wittg: BB 66.
55 Watts 68–9.
56 See above p. 35.
57 Wittg: BB 68.
58 Cf. Malcolm N. 'Knowledge of Other Minds', *Journal of Philosophy*, LV (1958) 978 (p. 383 in Pitcher: W).
59 Conze: BTI 257 (citing Vasubandhu).
60 LS 153–4.
61 LS 123.
62 Conze: BTI 133.

6 *Two 'Mental Acts'*

1 See Passmore 234.
2 Russell: M & L 191–2.
3 Stcherbatsky: CBN 39.
4 Stcherbatsky: BL I, 143–4.
5 VM. XIV, 135.
6 See e.g. Russell: A of M, 285.
7 A. III, 415.
8 MK 17: 2, 3.
9 Murti 168.
10 MK 20:2.
11 MK 20:4.
12 MK 1:5.
13 Ryle 77–8.
14 Wittg: BB 150.
15 Wittg: BB 151–2.
16 Wittg: BB 155.
17 Wittg: P.I. 614.
18 Wittg: P.I. 615.
19 MK 20:20.
20 Wittg: BB 151–2.
21 Wittg: P.I. 116.
22 MK 24:18.
23 MK 24:36.
24 MK 24:14.
25 MK 24:16, 17.
26 MK 17:21.
27 MK 24:37.
28 Shibles 85.
29 Wittg: P.I. 402.
30 V.P. 23.
31 V.P. 30b.
32 See above p. 24.
33 Jayatilleke s.718 f.
34 E.g. Russell: Probs 211.
35 Russell: Probs 197.
36 Russell: Probs 199.
37 Russell: M & L 210.
38 Russell: Probs 65.
39 E.g. Russell: Probs 147–8.
40 Russell: M & L 210.
41 See above p. 21.
42 Wittg: P.I. 187.
43 Wittg: BB 142.
44 Wittg: BB 27.
45 Robinson 110.
46 MK 3:6.
47 MK 3:9.
48 Robinson 124.
49 Robinson 125.
50 Robinson 126.
51 Suv. 7a.
52 Quoted at Murti 214.
53 Streng 83.
54 Aṣṭa 173–4.

7 *Ethics and Religion*

1 Moore viii.
2 See Gudmunsen: BM chs 3 and 4.
3 Artingstoll 17.
4 See above pp. 10–14.
5 For instance: Monier-Williams (1890) 123; Veinié (1892) 25; Tisdall (1903) 118; Bernard (1906) 54–5; Rao (1911) 317; Aung (1911) 107–8; PTSD (1921–5) 326; Ward (1923) 13; – and more recently – Wijesekera (1956) 59; Smart (1958) 190; Sharma (1965) 169; Saddhatissa (1970) 19.
6 Gudmunsen: EGW 317.
7 E.g. D. II, 84.
8 M. I, 149.
9 D. I, 3.
10 Sn. 900.
11 VM I, 159.
12 Mil. 34.
13 E.g. Dh. 39. 267, 412; Sn. 520, 636, 790; M.I.135.

14 K.V. xix, 6.
15 P. 266.
16 Matics 97.
17 Rees 24.
18 See Wittg. BB 81.
19 Wittg: LAPR 2.
20 Śatasāhasrikā 1466–9 (tr. Conze: SPW 75).
21 Suv. 68–9.
22 Saptaśatikā 202–5.
23 Suv. 57a.
24 See above p. 43.
25 Suv. 8a.
26 Pears: W 174.
27 Wittg: LAPR 53–4.
28 Wittg: LAPR 58.
29 Streng 169.
30 Streng 159–60.
31 Hick 23.
32 Wittg: P.I. 144.
33 Wittg: Z 461.
34 Wittg: LAPR 55.
35 Ibid.
36 Streng 159–60
37 Aṣṭa 177.
38 Hick 24.
39 Hick 27.
40 Pears: W 170–1.
41 Aṣṭa 365.
42 Aṣṭa 170.
43 Aṣṭa 39.
44 Aṣṭa 7.
45 Wittg: LAPR 70–1.
46 Wittg: LAPR 71.
47 MK 22:15.
48 See Grimm 391.
49 Jayatilleke s.794.
50 Ibid. (=Warder 57).

8 *Disconnection and Connection*

1 Gardiner 293–4.
2 Conze: TYBS 222.
3 Ibid.
4 Schopenhauer: WWI II, 371.
5 See e.g. Schopenhauer: WWI III, 308.
6 Gardiner 168–9.
7 See Conze: TYBS 223.
8 Schopenhauer: Werke IV, 130–1
9 von Wright 539.
10 E.g. VM.

Abbreviations and Bibliography

A. *Anguttara Nikāya* (tr. by F. L. Woodward and E. M. Hare as *Gradual Sayings*, 5 vols., 1932–6).

A.K. *Abhidharmakośa* by Vasubandhu, tr. by L. de la Vallée Poussin, 6 vols. (1923–31).

Artingstoll Artingstoll, T. M., 'Is Existentialism Buddhism?', *Hibbert Journal*, 63 (1964) 17.

Asl. *Atthasālini* (tr. by Pe Maung Tin and C. A. F. Rhys Davids as *The Expositor*, 2 vols., 1920–1).

Aṣṭa *Aṣṭasāhasrikā Prajñāpāramitā* (tr. by E. Conze as *The Perfection of Wisdom in Eight Thousand Lines*, Bolinas, 1973).

Aung Aung, S. Z., 'The Theory of Buddhist Ethics', *The Buddhist Review*, 3 (1911) 107–8.

Ayer Ayer, A. J., *Russell and Moore: The Analytical Heritage* (1971).

Bambrough Bambrough, R., 'Universals and Family Resemblances' P.A.S., 1960–1 (page nos. as reprinted in Pitcher: PW).

Bartley Bartley, W. W., *Wittgenstein* (1974).

BCA *Bodhicaryāvatāra* by Śāntideva (tr. in Matics).

Bernard Bernard, E. R., *Great Moral Teachers* (1906).

Conze: BTI Conze, E., *Buddhist Thought in India* (1962).

Conze: BWB Conze, E., *Buddhist Wisdom Books* (1958).

Conze: SPT Conze, E., *The Short Prajñāpāramitā Texts* (1973).

Conze: SPW Conze, E., *Selected Sayings from the Perfection of Wisdom* (1968).

Conze: TYBS Conze, E., *Thirty Years of Buddhist Studies* (1967).

D. *Dīgha Nikāya* (tr. by T. W. Rhys Davids as *Dialogues of the Buddha*, 3 vols., 1899–1921).

Dh. *Dhammapada*, tr. by Radhakrishnan (1950).

Edgerton Edgerton, F., *Buddhist Hybrid Sanskrit Grammar and Dictionary* (1953).

Fann Fann, K. T., *Wittgenstein's Conception of Philosophy* (1969).

Feyerabend Feyerabend, P., 'Wittgenstein's *Philosophical Investigations*' *Philosophical Review*, LXIV (1955) 449.

Gardiner Gardiner, P., *Schopenhauer* (1963).

Grimm Grimm, G., *The Doctrine of the Buddha*, 2nd ed. (1958).

Gudmunsen: BM Gudmunsen, C., 'Buddhist Metaethics', unpublished M.Phil. thesis, Univ. of London (1973).

Gudmunsen: EGW Gudmunsen, C., 'Ethics Gets in the Way', *Religious Studies*, 8 (1972) 311–18.
Guenther Guenther, H. V., *Buddhist Philosophy in Theory and Practice* (1972).
Har-Dayal Har-Dayal, *The Bodhisattva Doctrine in Buddhist Sanskrit Literature* (1932).
Hick Hick, J. H., 'Religious Faith as Experiencing- As', *Royal Institute of Philosophy Lectures*, 2 (1967–8).
Jager Jager, R., *The Development of Bertrand Russell's Philosophy* (1972).
Janik and Toulmin Janik, A. and Toulmin, S. E., *Wittgenstein's Vienna* (1973).
Jayatilleke Jayatilleke, K. N., *Early Buddhist Theory of Knowledge* (1963) (quoted by section number).
Johansson Johansson, R., *The Psychology of Nirvāṇa* (1969).
Kenny Kenny, A., *Wittgenstein* (1973).
K.V. Kathāvatthu (tr. by Aung S. Z. as *Points of Controversy*, 1915).
LS *Lankāvatāra Sutra*, tr. by D. T. Suzuki (1932).
M. *Majjhima Nikāya* (tr. by I. B. Horner as *Middle Length Sayings*, 3 vols., 1954–9).
Malcolm Malcolm, N., *Ludwig Wittgenstein: A Memoir* (1958).
Matics Matics, M. L., *Entering the Path of Enlightenment* (1971).
Mil. *Milindapañhā* (tr. by I. B. Horner as *Milinda's Questions*, 2 vols., 1964).
MK *Mādhyamikakārikās* by Nagarjuna, tr. in Streng.
MKV *Mādhyamikakārikāvṛtti* by Candrakīrti (commentary on MK).
Monier-Williams Monier-Williams, M., *Buddhism* (1890).
Moore Moore, G. E., *Principia Ethica* (1903).
Mundle Mundle, C. W. K., *Perception: Facts and Theories* (1971).
Murti Murti, T. R. V., *The Central Philosophy of Buddhism* (1955).
P. *Pañcaviṃśatisāhasrika Prajñāpāramitā*.
P.A.S. *Proceedings of the Aristotelian Society*.
Passmore Passmore, J., *A Hundred Years of Philosophy* (Penguin, 1968).
Pears: BR & BT Pears, D., *Bertrand Russell and the British Tradition in Philosophy* (1967).
Pears: W Pears, D., *Wittgenstein* (1971).
Pitcher: PW Pitcher, G. W., *The Philosophy of Wittgenstein* (Englewood Cliffs, 1964).
Pitcher: W Pitcher, G. W. (ed.), *Wittgenstein: The Philosophical Investigations* (London, 1968).
PTSD *Pāli Text Society Dictionary*, eds W. Stede and T. W. Rhys Davids (1925).

Rao Rao, K. G., 'The Significance of the Buddhistic Ethic', *The Westminster Review*, 176 (1911).

Rees Rees, R., 'Some Developments in Wittgenstein's View of Ethics', *Philosophical Review*, 74 (1965) 24 (quoting unnamed 1945 works or conversations of Wittgenstein).

Robinson Robinson, R. H., *Early Mādhyamika in India and China* (Wisconsin, 1967).

Russell: A of M Russell, B., *The Analysis of Mind* (1921).

Russell: M & L Russell, B., *Mysticism and Logic* (1917).

Russell: Ph.L.A. Russell, B., *The Philosophy of Logical Atomism* (1918) (page nos. as in D. Pears, *Russell's Logical Atomism* 1972).

Russell: Probs Russell, B., *The Problems of Philosophy* (1912).

Ryle Ryle, G., *The Concept of Mind* (1949).

S. *Saṃyutta Nikāya* (tr. by C. A. F. Rhys Davids and F. L. Woodward as *Kindred Sayings*, 5 vols., 1916–30).

Saddhatissa Saddhatissa, H., *Buddhist Ethics* (1970).

Saptaśatikā Saptaśatikā Prajñāpāramitā (tr. in Conze: SPT as 'The Perfection of Wisdom in 700 Lines').

Schilpp Schilpp, P. (ed.), *The Philosophy of Bertrand Russell* (1944).

Schopenhauer: Werke Schopenhauer, A., *Sämtliche Werke* (Leipzig, 1938).

Schopenhauer: WWI Schopenhauer, A., *The World as Will and Idea*, tr. by R. B. Haldane and J. Kemp (1883; 10th impr., 1957).

Sharma Sharma, I. C., *Ethical Philosophies of India* (1965).

Shibles Shibles, W. A., *Wittgenstein, Language and Philosophy* (Iowa, 1969).

Smart Smart, N., *Reasons and Faiths* (1958).

Sn. *Sutta Nipāta* (tr. by E. M. Hare as *Woven Cadences*, 1945).

S.P. Śatasahāsrikā Prajñāpāramitā, extracts tr. in Conze: SPW.

Stcherbatsky: BL Stcherbatsky, Th., *Buddhist Logic*, 2 vols. (reprinted New York, 1962).

Stcherbatsky: CBN Stcherbatsky, Th., *The Conception of Buddhist Nirvāṇa* (Leningrad, 1927).

Stcherbatsky: CCB Stcherbatsky, Th., *The Central Conception of Buddhism and the Meaning of the Word 'Dharma'* (Delhi, 1970; first published 1923).

Streng Streng, F. J., *Emptiness: A Study in Religious Meaning* (Nashville, 1967).

Suv. *Suvikrāntavikrāmiparipṛcchā*, tr. in Conze: SPT.

Tisdall Tisdall, St Clair, W., *The Noble Eightfold Path* (1903).

Ud. *Udāna* (tr. by F. L. Woodward as *Verses of Uplift*, 1948).

van Peursen van Peursen, C. A., *Ludwig Wittgenstein: An Introduction to his Philosophy*, tr. Rex Ambler (1969).

Veinié Veinié, C., *La Morale du Bouddha et la Morale du Christ* (Geneva, 1892).

VM *Visuddhimagga* by Buddhaghosa (tr. by Nyānamoli as *The Path of Purification*, Colombo, 1964).

von Wright von Wright, G. H., 'Wittgenstein: A Biographical Sketch', *Philosophical Review*, LXIV (1955).

V.P. *Vajracchedikā Prajñāpāramitā*, tr. in Conze: BWB and Conze: SPT.

VV *Vigrahavyāvartanī* (tr. as 'Averting the Arguments' in Streng).

Ward Ward, C. H. S., *The Ethics of Gotama Buddha* (Colombo, 1923).

Warder Warder, A. K., 'Early Buddhism and Other Contemporary Systems', *Bulletin of the School of Oriental and African Studies* (1956).

Watts Watts, A. W., *Psychotherapy East and West* (1961).

Wijesekara Wijesekara, O. H. de A., 'Buddhist Ethics' in *Pathways of Buddhist Thought*, ed. Nyānaponika (1971).

Wittg: BB Wittgenstein, L., *The Blue and Brown Books*, 2nd edit. (1969).

Wittg: LAPR Wittgenstein, L., *Lectures and Conversations on Aesthetics, Psychology and Religious Belief* (Oxford, 1966).

Wittg: PB Wittgenstein, L., *Philosophische Bemerkungen* (Oxford, 1964).

Wittg: PESD 'Wittgenstein's Notes for Lectures on "Private Experience" and "Sense-Data"', ed. R. Rees, *Philosophical Review*, LXXVII (1968) (page nos. as reprinted in *The Private Language Argument*, ed. O. R. Jones, 1971).

Wittg: P.I. Wittgenstein, L., *Philosophical Investigations* (1953), tr. by G. E. M. Anscombe (part I quoted by section no.; part II by page no.).

Wittg: TLP Wittgenstein, L., *Tractatus Logico-Philosophicus*, tr. by D. F. Pears and B. F. McGuiness (1961).

Wittg: Z Wittgenstein, L., *Zettel*, ed. G. E. M. Anscombe and G. H. von Wright; tr. by G. E. M. Anscombe (Oxford, 1967).

Index